MW00997926

Afternoon Tea

Afternoon Tea

DELICIOUS RECIPES *for* SCONES, SAVORIES *&* SWEETS

hm|books

EDITOR *Lorna Reeves*
CREATIVE DIRECTOR/PHOTOGRAPHY *Mac Jamieson*
ART DIRECTOR *Cailyn Haynes*
ASSOCIATE EDITOR *Betty Terry*
COPY EDITOR *Nancy Ogburn*
EDITORIAL ASSISTANT *Amy Hannum*
STYLIST *Lucy Wilson Herndon*
SENIOR PHOTOGRAPHER *Marcy Black Simpson, John O'Hagan*
PHOTOGRAPHERS *Sarah Arrington, Kamin H. Williams*
TEST KITCHEN DIRECTOR *Janice Ritter*
TEST KITCHEN PROFESSIONAL *Janet Lambert*
SENIOR DIGITAL IMAGING SPECIALIST *Delisa McDaniel*
DIGITAL IMAGING SPECIALIST *Clark Densmore*

PRESIDENT *Phyllis Hoffman DePiano*
EXECUTIVE VICE PRESIDENT/COO *Eric W. Hoffman*
EXECUTIVE VICE PRESIDENT/CCO *Brian Hart Hoffman*
EXECUTIVE VICE PRESIDENT/CFO *G. Marc Neas*
VICE PRESIDENT/FINANCE *Michael Adams*
VICE PRESIDENT/MANUFACTURING *Greg Baugh*
VICE PRESIDENT/EDITORIAL *Cindy Smith Cooper*
VICE PRESIDENT/CONSUMER MARKETING *Silvia Rider*
VICE PRESIDENT/ADMINISTRATION *Lynn Lee Terry*

Copyright © 2013 by Hoffman Media, LLC
Publishers of *TeaTime* magazine
teatimemagazine.com

All rights reserved. No part of this book may be reproduced or
transmitted in any form or by any means, electronic or mechanical,
including photocopying, or by any information storage and
retrieval system, without permission in writing from Hoffman
Media, LLC. Reviewers may quote brief passages.

First published in 2013 by Hoffman Media, LLC
Birmingham, Alabama
With offices at
1900 International Park Drive, Suite 50
Birmingham, Alabama 35243
hoffmanmedia.com

ISBN 978-0-9770069-5-3
Printed in Mexico

ON THE COVER: SCONES: Almond-Ginger Scones (page 26),
Raspberries and Cream Scones (page 65) SAVORIES: Spicy Beef
Finger Sandwiches (page 19), Curried Smoked Turkey Salad
Sandwiches (page 44), Smoked Trout Tea Sandwiches (page 79)
SWEETS: Mini Pound Cakes (page 30), Lemon French Macarons
(page 101), German Chocolate–Mascarpone Tartlets (page 117).
Recipe development and food styling by Janet Lambert
Photography by Marcy Black Simpson
Photo styling by Lucy W. Herndon

Contents

Introduction

THERE'S SOMETHING ABOUT A THREE-TIERED STAND that makes afternoon tea memorable. Perhaps it's the appeal of having within easy reach a tower filled with delectable foods to be leisurely savored while sipping a cup of tea. Or maybe it's the elegance and formality the stand lends to the occasion. There's also the convenience of being able to serve all the courses at once, which allows the hostess to focus fully on her guests and engage in meaningful conversation.

Yet, it hasn't always been easy to find tiered stands. Though ubiquitous in the Victorian and Edwardian eras, as Jane Pettigrew tells us in the chapter about their history, these tri-level servers fell out of favor for many decades until afternoon tea regained popularity in the late 20th century. Nowadays, with the resurgence of teatime, tiered stands are making a comeback.

The menus within these pages are suitable for such servers and for the most-celebrated special occasions. Additional recipes for scones, savories, and sweets appear in subsequent chapters. These can be used to further enhance the menus or to create combinations tailored to your guests' preferences or to the theme of the event.

To accompany these delightful treats, you may serve the teas recommended in the pairings for each course of the menus or select your own favorites. Our guidelines for steeping tea explain how to prepare the various types and give tips for successful infusions.

Whether your tiered stand is a family heirloom handed down through many generations or one assembled from stacked pedestal cake stands of varying sizes is not as important as the memories you will make with your guests around the table as you enjoy afternoon tea.

THE *Three-Tier* CAKE STAND

BY JANE PETTIGREW

TODAY'S TEA TABLES ALMOST ALWAYS FEATURE A TIERED CAKE STAND that elegantly displays an eye-catching array of mouthwatering sandwiches, scones, and pastries. We perhaps assume that these graceful silver and porcelain stands have always played a part on traditional tea tables. And as we lovingly prepare each tier and garnish the food with flowers and fruits, we may ponder how our great-grandmothers, great-great-aunts, and generations of teatime hostesses before them would have arranged theirs.

But it is, in fact, unlikely that Victorian ladies who served tea before the 1880s used such stands on their tea tables. The cakes and pastries were probably brought to the table in silver baskets or on glass or porcelain platters that stood modestly on a pedestal just above the height of the other dishes. According to researchers in The Goldsmiths' Company's library, "Historically, silversmiths would have made 'cake baskets' or 'bread baskets' for the presentation of scones, muffins, and cakes. In our catalogue, we have sources on silver baskets, but there is nothing

for cake stands, nor are cake stands mentioned in dictionaries of silver."

However, Georgian and Victorian diners would have been very familiar with silver, pressed glass, crystal, or porcelain single-tier cake stands, known originally as salvers and used to display wedding cakes and fancy desserts. These sat on either a solid base approximately 6 inches high or a pedestal that created a theatrical effect and showed the cake off to its best advantage. Some of the grander, solid-silver salvers had a mechanism that allowed them to revolve slowly, while others contained fun novelty features such as musical boxes!

Victorian dinner tables often also held quite elaborate centerpieces called "epergnes," which included branches of various sizes positioned at different heights and designed to hold salt and pepper dishes and trays of sweetmeats or fruit. And in most drawing rooms of that period, a folding mahogany or oak cake stand 2 or 3 feet tall would have stood on the floor beside the tea table or trolley. These had hinged trays that dropped down to hold platefuls of toasted

muffins and hot buttered crumpets but then folded neatly away once tea was over. The stands continued to play their part at teatime, both in Britain and North America, and in the 1922 edition of Emily Post's *Etiquette* (published in the United States), we read, "... on the tea-table, back of the tray, or on shelves of a separate 'curate,' a stand made of three small shelves, each just big enough for one good-sized plate, are always two, usually three, varieties of cake and hot breads." So, perhaps, as afternoon tea gained favor in the later years of the 19th century, the pedestal cake platters; the decorative, space-saving epergnes; and the floor-standing wooden cake stands gradually merged to create a multitiered stand designed specifically for the display of irresistible cakes and pastries on the tea table.

According to catalogues and silver specialists, the earliest plated-silver cake stands were manufactured in the 1880s and '90s, and by the time tea reached its Edwardian heyday, they were widely available for use both in the home and in hotel lounges. The London department store Jas. Shoolbred & Co. Ltd., in its 1912 to 1914 catalogue, offered "Brass Cake Stands (These can also be supplied in Copper or Silver Oxidized)." Customers could choose between the "Polished Brass, 2ft 6in. high 14/-" and

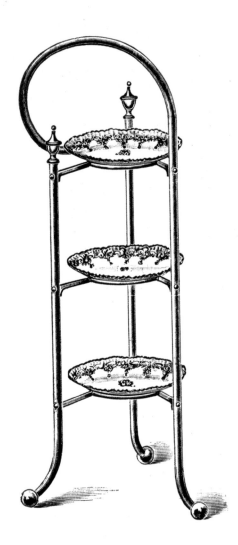

Brass cake stand from a catalogue published by Jas. Shoolbred & Co., circa 1915. (© The Geffrye, Museum of the Home)

During the Edwardian era (1901 to 1910), even a less formal tea in the garden would have included a three-tier cake stand and a maid to serve tea, such as this photograph taken circa 1905. (Photo by G.T. Jones & Son/Sean Sexton/Getty Images)

"Polished Brass, plates extra, 2ft 8in. high 21/-." These rather tall stands were presumably intended for use on sideboards and buffet tables at tea receptions catering to a large number of guests. Smaller stands, designed for use on the tea table itself, stood only 14, 15, or 16 inches tall, and antiques dealers offer these today as "Victorian silver plated three-tier cake stand in a frame with removable oval pierced-edged plates made in ca 1890. Height 15.75 inches, width 28 inches, depth 7 inches" and "Antique Edwardian silver plated three-tier cake stand, having a graduated suite of three removable octagonal plates with applied leaf borders, sitting within a very pretty tapering frame with scroll-work handle and feet, made in Sheffield in ca 1910." Hostesses who wished to coordinate their cake display with the chosen tea set could, of course, replace the silver trays with matching porcelain cake plates.

Through the first 30 years or so of the 20th century, cake stands came into their own, and books on etiquette began to advise their use on the tea table. Mrs. Massey Lyon wrote in her 1927 publication, *Etiquette*: "In towns, the tea

The buffet table at a reception for the graduation ceremony for women students at King's College Medical School, circa 1918, is laden with delicious savories, scones, and sweets on tiered stands. (Photo by Topical Press Agency)

tray is put upon a small table, brought out from the side of the room for the purpose, and covered with a lace-trimmed or embroidered cloth, and cakes, etc., are disposed on the table if large enough, on a tiered cake stand, or whatever convenience suggests. Where a hostess is usually 'on her own' for tea [i.e., without her maid], one of the tiny tiered stands which take their place upon the table prove most convenient and they enable her to pass three or four things at once to her guests." In 1905, Goldsmiths' and Silversmiths' Company, London, offered just such a miniature stand of "circular tiers with leaf capped supports and a bud finial, height 15.5 cm 6 inches, weight 3 oz."

By the 1930s and '40s, stands were being manufactured not just in silver and silver plate, but also in chrome, etched glass, and modern, colorful materials such as Perspex and Bakelite. Most middle- and upper-class homes would have owned at least one stand of a style and design to suit the décor and the hostess's individual preference. But in the 1950s, as afternoon tea faded into the shadows (to be replaced by convenience foods and instant coffee), so, too, did cakes stands, and when the tea renaissance of the 1990s sent out its first ripples, it was almost impossible to find new ones. Tea lovers scoured antiques markets to salvage what was left from earlier days, but it took another 15 to 20 years for the silversmiths and porcelain companies to once again produce elegant silver and porcelain stands.

Tea lovers often ask how traditional tea foods should be arranged on the stand's three tiers, and the honest answer is that there are no rules. However, some tearooms and hotel lounges choose to arrange the little sandwiches on the lowest tier, the scones in the middle, and the tiny, tempting, outrageously wicked pastries on the top, where they create quite a show. Those who are concerned that scones should be brought to the table while still warm from the oven place dishes of jam, butter, and clotted cream on the middle tier and deliver the scones to the table only when guests are ready. Others prefer to offer the warm scones as the first course and, therefore, place them on the bottom tier and savories on the middle one. It is the personal choices and individual creative touches to the tiered stand that make teatime such a timeless pleasure.

Jane Pettigrew is an international tea expert, who has written 14 books on the subject, including the new edition of *A Social History of Tea*, published by Benjamin Press. A former tearoom owner, she is a much-sought-after consultant to tea businesses and hotels, a conference speaker, and a tea educator. Although her travels take her around the globe, she resides in London.

SCONE

Fontina, Parmesan, and Roasted Red Pepper Scones
Simpson & Vail's Blue Moon Black Tea

SAVORIES

Strawberry-Basil Tea Hearts
Petite Crab Cakes with Mango Chutney
Spicy Beef Finger Sandwiches
Margaret's Hope Second Flush Darjeeling Black Tea

SWEETS

Pink Heart Shortbread Cookies
Mini Chocolate Cheesecakes
Raspberry-Pistachio Tartlets
Simpson & Vail's Red Velvet Cupcake Tea

Valentine's DAY

Fontina, Parmesan, and Roasted Red Pepper Scones

Yield: 12 scones
Preparation: 25 minutes
Bake: 15 minutes

1¾ cups self-rising flour
⅛ teaspoon ground black pepper
3 tablespoons cold salted butter, cut into pieces
½ cup coarsely shredded fontina cheese
½ cup finely grated Parmesan cheese*
¼ cup very finely chopped roasted red pepper
1 cup plus 1 tablespoon heavy whipping cream, divided
1 recipe Smoked Paprika Butter (recipe follows)

• Preheat oven to 400°.
• Spray 2 (6-well) heart-shaped pans† with nonstick baking spray with flour. Set aside.
• In a medium bowl, combine flour and black pepper, whisking well. Using a pastry blender, cut butter into flour mixture until mixture resembles coarse crumbs. Add cheeses and roasted red pepper, tossing to coat with flour. Add 1 cup cream, stirring until mixture comes together as a dough. (If mixture seems dry, add more cream, 1 tablespoon at a time, until uniformly moist.)
• Using a levered 3-tablespoon scoop, drop dough into wells of prepared pans, patting dough to create a level surface. Brush dough with remaining 1 table-spoon cream.
• Bake until scones are light golden brown and a wooden pick inserted in the centers comes out clean, approximately 15 minutes.
• Serve warm with Smoked Paprika Butter, if desired.

A fine Microplane grater will make quick work of grating Parmesan cheese, and the fine shreds it produces will melt easily. We do not recommend using preshredded Parmesan; it will not melt as well.

†*We used Nordicware Platinum Mini Heart Baking Pans, which are available online at nordicware.com.*

Smoked Paprika Butter

Yield: ½ cup
Preparation: 5 minutes

½ cup salted butter, at room temperature
½ teaspoon smoked paprika

• In a small bowl, combine butter and paprika, stirring until thoroughly blended. Pipe or decoratively swirl butter into a serving dish.

MAKE-AHEAD TIP: *Smoked Paprika Butter may be made a day in advance, covered, and refrigerated. Let come to room temperature before serving.*

Strawberry-Basil Tea Hearts

Yield: 16 finger sandwiches
Preparation: 25 minutes
Refrigerate: 1 hour

4 ounces cream cheese, softened
1 teaspoon heavy whipping cream
¼ cup very finely minced fresh strawberries
2 teaspoons finely minced fresh basil
⅛ teaspoon ground black pepper
16 slices very thin white bread, such as Pepperidge Farm

• In a small bowl, combine cream cheese and cream. Beat at medium speed with an electric mixer until smooth and creamy. Add strawberries, basil, and pepper, stirring by hand until incorporated. Refrigerate mixture for 1 hour before using.
• Using a 2-inch heart-shaped cutter, cut 32 hearts from bread. Using a smaller heart-shaped cutter, cut out hearts from center of 16 larger hearts, discarding cutouts.
• Transfer cream cheese mixture to a piping bag fitted with a small open-star tip (Wilton #32). Pipe mixture onto uncut bread hearts, outlining edge of bread and then filling in center. Top with cut bread hearts so that mixture shows through. Cover sandwiches with damp paper towels, and refrigerate, covered, until ready to serve. (Sandwiches may be made earlier in the day.)

on paper towels. Place crab cakes on a rimmed baking sheet lined with parchment paper.
• Bake until hot, 3 to 5 minutes.
• Spread ½ teaspoon chutney onto each cracker. Top with a crab cake.
• Garnish with a mango heart and a chive, if desired.
• Serve immediately.

To make mango hearts, use a very small heart-shaped cutter to cut heart shapes from slices of mango. We used Del Monte SunFresh mango.

MAKE-AHEAD TIP: *Crab cakes may be rolled in panko and shaped, then covered and refrigerated until ready to sauté.*

Petite Crab Cakes with Mango Chutney
Yield: 23 crab cakes
Preparation: 30 minutes
Cook: 4 minutes
Bake: 5 minutes

1 (8-ounce) container pasteurized lump crabmeat
1 large egg, lightly beaten
1½ cups panko (Japanese bread crumbs), divided
2 tablespoons minced shallot
1 tablespoon minced fresh chives
1 tablespoon minced fresh parsley
1 tablespoon fresh lemon juice
2 teaspoons Dijon-style mustard
¼ teaspoon salt
¼ teaspoon ground black pepper
⅓ cup olive oil
½ cup hot mango chutney, such as Major Grey's
23 almond rice crackers, such as Blue Diamond
Garnish: mango hearts* and fresh chives

• Preheat oven to 350°.
• In a medium bowl, combine crabmeat, egg, ¼ cup panko, shallot, chives, parsley, lemon juice, mustard, salt, and pepper, stirring to blend. Using a levered 2-teaspoon scoop, drop crab mixture into remaining 1¼ cups panko, tossing to coat. Shape into patties.
• In a large sauté pan, heat olive oil over medium-high heat. Cook crab cakes in batches, 1 to 2 minutes per side, until crumbs are medium golden brown. (Reduce heat to medium if crab cakes brown too quickly.) Drain

Spicy Beef Finger Sandwiches
Yield: 8 finger sandwiches
Preparation: 45 minutes
Marinate: 30 minutes
Cook: 4 minutes
Bake: 5 to 7 minutes

¼ teaspoon smoked paprika
¼ teaspoon chili powder
¼ teaspoon ground cumin
⅛ teaspoon garlic salt
⅛ teaspoon ground black pepper
⅛ teaspoon ground red pepper
1 (6-ounce) beef fillet
3 teaspoons olive oil, divided
1 recipe Lime-Cilantro Butter (recipe follows)
16 (3-x-1-inch) toasted French bread slices, crusts trimmed
Arugula leaves
Garnish: grape tomato slices

• Preheat oven to 350°.
• Line a baking sheet with aluminum foil. Set aside.
• In a small bowl, combine paprika, chili powder, cumin, garlic salt, black pepper, and red pepper, mixing well. Season beef fillet with spice mixture on both sides. Drizzle each side with 1 teaspoon olive oil, rubbing spices and oil into beef. Let sit at room temperature for 30 minutes to marinate.
• In a small sauté pan, heat remaining 1 teaspoon olive oil over medium-high heat. When oil shimmers, add fillet, and sear on all sides until deep brown, approximately 2 minutes per side. Place on prepared baking sheet.
• Bake for 5 to 7 minutes for rare, longer for a greater degree of doneness. (Fillet will feel very springy when pressed with a finger after cooking for a short time; this indicates a rare interior. If meat feels very firm when

pressed, it is more well done.) Remove pan from oven, and wrap fillet in foil. Let rest for 15 minutes. Thinly slice beef (approximately ⅛ inch thick) across the grain.
• Spread Lime-Cilantro Butter on one side of bread slices. Lay a leaf of arugula on each of 8 bread slices. Ruffle a slice of beef on top of arugula. Top with another bread slice, butter side down.
• Garnish each sandwich with 3 slices grape tomato, if desired.
• Serve immediately.

MAKE-AHEAD TIP: *Beef fillet can be cooked in advance, and refrigerated for up to a day. Before serving, heat in a 350° oven just until warm, approximately 5 minutes.*

Lime-Cilantro Butter

Yield: ¼ cup
Preparation: 5 minutes

¼ cup salted butter, softened
½ teaspoon fresh lime zest
1 teaspoon fresh lime juice
1 tablespoon finely chopped fresh cilantro

• In a small bowl, combine butter, lime zest, lime juice, and cilantro, stirring until blended.

MAKE-AHEAD TIP: *Butter may be made a day in advance and refrigerated in a covered container. Let come to room temperature before serving.*

thickness. Using a 2-inch heart-shaped cutter, cut 48 hearts from dough, rerolling scraps as necessary. Place cookies on prepared baking sheets, and refrigerate for 15 minutes. (This will help cookies retain their shape while baking.)

• Bake cookies until a few edges are just beginning to turn very light brown, approximately 13 minutes. Remove from baking sheet, and let cool completely on a wire rack.

• Dust cooled cookies with confectioners' sugar, if desired.

• Store in an airtight container, and use within 3 days.

MAKE AHEAD TIP: *Cookies can be baked in advance and frozen for up to 1 week. Dust with confectioners' sugar just before serving.*

Mini Chocolate Cheesecakes

Yield: 12 mini cheesecakes
Preparation: 35 minutes
Bake: 8 minutes
Cool: 1 hour
Refrigerate: 4 hours

1 cup chocolate wafer cookie crumbs, such as
    Nabisco Famous Chocolate Wafers
7 tablespoons sugar, divided
4 tablespoons salted butter, melted
4 ounces cream cheese, softened
3 tablespoons natural unsweetened cocoa powder
1 large egg
½ teaspoon vanilla extract
1 recipe Chocolate Ganache (recipe follows)
Garnish: 12 cherries with stems

• Preheat oven to 350°.

• Spray a 12-well square mini cheesecake pan with nonstick cooking spray. Set aside.

• In a small bowl, combine cookie crumbs, 1 table-spoon sugar, and melted butter, stirring until blended. Firmly and evenly press 2 teaspoons crumb mixture into the bottom of each well of prepared pan. Set aside.

• In a medium bowl, beat cream cheese at medium speed with an electric mixer until smooth and creamy. Gradually add remaining 6 tablespoons sugar and cocoa, beating until incorporated. Add egg and vanilla extract, beating until incorporated. Using a levered 1½-tablespoon scoop, drop cream-cheese mixture onto cookie crumb base in each well of pan, smoothing to create a level surface.

• Bake until cheesecakes are slightly puffed, approxi-mately 8 minutes. Let cool completely in pan on a wire rack. Cover pan, and refrigerate for at least 4 hours or overnight.

Pink Heart Shortbread Cookies

Yield: 48 cookies
Preparation: 35 minutes
Bake: 13 minutes
Refrigerate: 1¼ hours

2 cups all-purpose flour
¼ teaspoon salt
1 cup salted butter, softened
½ cup confectioners' sugar
½ teaspoon vanilla extract
½ teaspoon almond extract
Red paste food coloring, such as Wilton
Garnish: confectioners' sugar

• In a medium bowl, combine flour and salt, whisking well. Set aside.

• In a large bowl, combine butter, confectioners' sugar, vanilla extract, and almond extract. Beat at high speed with an electric mixer until light and creamy. Add food coloring until desired shade of pink is achieved. Gradually add flour mixture to butter mixture, beating until combined. Wrap dough well in plastic wrap, and refrigerate for 1 hour.

• Preheat oven to 350°.

• Line 2 rimmed baking sheets with parchment paper. Set aside.

• On a lightly floured surface, roll dough to a ¼-inch

- Remove cheesecakes from pan. Spoon 2 teaspoons Chocolate Ganache onto each cheesecake.
- Garnish each with a cherry, if desired.

MAKE-AHEAD TIP: *Cheesecakes may be made in advance, wrapped tightly while still in the pan, and frozen for up to a week. Top with ganache and cherries just before serving.*

Chocolate Ganache
Yield: ½ cup
Preparation: 5 minutes

¼ cup heavy whipping cream
½ cup dark chocolate morsels

- In a small saucepan, scald cream over medium heat, being careful not to let cream boil. Remove from heat, and add dark chocolate morsels. Let stand for 1 minute to melt morsels; stir to combine. Let cool slightly until somewhat thickened before using.

Raspberry-Pistachio Tartlets
Yield: 8 tartlets
Preparation: 1 hour
Refrigerate: 30 minutes
Bake: 12 minutes

1 (14.1-ounce) package refrigerated pie dough
  (2 sheets)
½ cup shelled roasted salted pistachios
⅓ cup sugar
4 tablespoons salted butter
1 large egg
1 tablespoon all-purpose flour
¼ teaspoon vanilla extract
2½ cups fresh raspberries
½ cup light corn syrup

- Preheat oven to 450°.
- On a floured surface, unroll both sheets of pie dough. Using a 4½-inch round cutter, cut 8 circles. Press dough into 8 (3¾-inch) tartlet pans with removable bottoms. Refrigerate for 30 minutes.
- Place tartlet pans on a rimmed baking sheet, and prick bottoms with a fork to prevent puffing during baking.
- Bake until very light golden brown, approximately 5 minutes. Let tartlet shells cool completely.
- Reduce oven temperature to 375°.
- In the work bowl of a food processor, pulse pistachios and sugar until finely ground. Add butter, 1 tablespoon at a time, pulsing to blend. Add egg, flour, and vanilla extract, pulsing until mixture is combined. Divide evenly among cooled tartlet shells.
- Bake until filling is slightly puffed, approximately 12 minutes. (Tartlets will fall as they cool.)
- Slice raspberries in half vertically, reserving 8 whole berries. Place a whole raspberry in the center of each tartlet. Arrange cut raspberries, cut side up, in concentric circles around whole raspberry. (Berries should resemble a flower.)
- Place corn syrup in a small microwave-proof bowl. Microwave on high at 10-second intervals until syrup is very warm and thin. Brush warm syrup over raspberries.
- Refrigerate tartlets until serving time, up to 4 hours.

MENU

SCONE
Almond-Ginger Scones
 *Capital Tea's Himalayan Gold Organic Black Tea*

SAVORIES
Mustard–Egg Salad Tea Sandwiches
Asparagus Canapés
Radish Slaw in Egg-Roll Baskets
Dragonwell Lung Ching Green Tea

SWEETS
Macadamia French Macarons
Mini Pound Cakes
Peanut Butter Mousse in Dark Chocolate Cups
Milk Oolong Tea

Easter

Almond-Ginger Scones

Yield: 21 scones
Preparation: 20 minutes
Bake: 8 minutes

2 cups all-purpose flour
⅓ cup sugar
1 tablespoon baking powder
2 teaspoons ground ginger
½ teaspoon salt
¼ teaspoon cream of tartar
3 tablespoons minced crystallized ginger, divided
6 tablespoons cold, salted butter, cut into pieces
⅓ cup plus 2 tablespoons toasted sliced almonds, divided
1 large egg
¾ cup cold heavy whipping cream, divided
¼ teaspoon almond extract

• Preheat oven to 400°.
• Line a rimmed baking sheet with parchment paper. Set aside.
• In a large bowl, combine flour, sugar, baking powder, ground ginger, salt, and cream of tartar, whisking well. Add 2 tablespoons crystallized ginger, stirring to combine. Using a pastry blender, cut butter into flour mixture until mixture resembles coarse crumbs. Add ⅓ cup almonds, stirring to combine. Set aside.
• In a measuring cup, combine egg, ½ cup plus 3 tablespoons cream, and almond extract, whisking well. Add egg mixture all at once to flour mixture, stirring to combine. (Mixture will be crumbly. However, if mixture seems dry, add more cream, 1 tablespoon at a time, until uniformly moist.) Bring dough together with hands to form a smooth ball. (Dough will be very stiff.)
• Turn dough out onto a lightly floured surface, and knead lightly 4 to 5 times. Using a floured rolling pin, roll dough to a ½-inch thickness. Using a 2¾-inch triangular cutter, cut 21 shapes from dough, rerolling scraps as necessary. Place scones 2 inches apart on prepared baking sheet.
• Brush tops with remaining 1 tablespoon cream, and sprinkle with remaining 2 tablespoons almonds and remaining 1 tablespoon crystallized ginger.
• Bake until edges of scones are golden brown and a wooden pick inserted in the centers comes out clean, 8 to 9 minutes.
• Serve warm.

Mustard-Egg Salad Tea Sandwiches

Yield: 20 tea sandwiches
Preparation: 25 minutes
Refrigerate: 4 hours

5 large hard-boiled eggs, finely chopped
1 tablespoon Dijon-style mustard
1 tablespoon mayonnaise
1 tablespoon sweet pickle relish
1 tablespoon minced celery
⅛ teaspoon salt
⅛ teaspoon ground black pepper
20 slices seedless rye bread
Garnish: watercress

• In a medium bowl, combine eggs, mustard, mayonnaise, pickle relish, celery, salt, and pepper, stirring well. Cover, and refrigerate until cold, approximately 4 hours.
• Using a 2½-x-1¾-inch egg-shaped cutter, cut shapes from bread. Toast on a griddle or under a broiler. Spread egg salad onto 10 bread slices, and top with remaining bread slices.
• Garnish with watercress, if desired.

MAKE-AHEAD TIP: *Egg salad can be made a day in advance and refrigerated until needed.*

KITCHEN TIP: *The same pastry blender you use to make scones is also great for chopping hard-boiled eggs.*

- Using a 1½-inch hexagonal cutter, cut 12 shapes from bread.
- Transfer cream cheese mixture to a piping bag fitted with a medium open tip (Wilton #12). Pipe onto bread, and smooth with an offset spatula. Arrange 3 asparagus tips on top of each bread slice to resemble a bouquet.
- Garnish with a lemon curl, if desired.
- Cover canapés with damp paper towels, place in an airtight container, and refrigerate for up to 4 hours.

Radish Slaw in Egg-Roll Baskets

Yield: 24 servings
Preparation: 30 minutes
Bake: 4 minutes

6 tablespoons olive oil, divided
8 refrigerated egg-roll wrappers
¼ cup fresh lemon juice
2 teaspoons sugar
2 teaspoons finely minced shallot
¼ teaspoon salt
⅛ teaspoon ground black pepper
1½ cups whole radishes
Garnish: purple radish microgreens

- Preheat oven to 400°.
- Brush wells of a 24-well mini muffin pan with 1 tablespoon olive oil.
- Using a 3-inch round cutter, cut 24 rounds from egg-roll wrappers. Brush surface of wrappers with 1 tablespoon olive oil. Lightly press into prepared wells of muffin pan, forming a ruffled basket shape.
- Bake until baskets are light golden brown and crisp, approximately 4 minutes. Transfer baskets to a wire rack, and let cool completely. Store in an airtight container until needed.
- In a small bowl, combine lemon juice, sugar, shallot, salt, and pepper, whisking to blend. Slowly add remaining 4 tablespoons olive oil, whisking until emulsified. Set aside.
- Trim any roots or green tops from radishes. Using a fine grater, grate radishes. Press into a fine-mesh sieve to extract as much liquid as possible. Place grated radishes in a bowl, and fluff with a fork.
- Place approximately 1 tablespoon grated radish in each basket. Drizzle with lemon vinaigrette.
- Garnish with purple radish microgreens, if desired.
- Serve immediately.

MAKE-AHEAD TIP: *Egg-roll baskets may be made a day in advance and stored in a airtight container. Radishes may be grated up to 4 hours in advance and refrigerated in a covered container until needed.*

Asparagus Canapés

Yield: 12 canapés
Preparation: 35 minutes
Bake: 5 minutes

36 tips very thin asparagus
½ teaspoon olive oil
¼ teaspoon salt, divided
4 ounces cream cheese, softened
2 teaspoons heavy whipping cream
2 teaspoons finely chopped fresh dill
1 teaspoon finely chopped fresh parsley
1 teaspoon fresh lemon zest
1 teaspoon fresh lemon juice
12 slices very thin wheat sandwich bread, such as
    Pepperidge Farm Very Thin Wheat
Garnish: lemon curls

- Preheat oven to 400°.
- Line a rimmed baking sheet with parchment paper.
- In a medium bowl, combine asparagus tips and olive oil, tossing to coat. Spread in a single layer on prepared baking sheet. Sprinkle with ⅛ teaspoon salt.
- Roast asparagus tips until crisp-tender, approximately 5 minutes. Let cool.
- In a small bowl, combine cream cheese and cream, Beat at high speed with an electric mixer until light and fluffy. Add dill, parsley, lemon zest, lemon juice, and remaining ⅛ teaspoon salt, stirring to combine. Set aside.

Macadamia French Macarons with Apricot-Mascarpone Filling

Yield: 37 sandwich cookies
Preparation: 5 hours
Bake: 20 minutes

3 large egg whites
1 cup salted macadamia nuts
2 cups confectioners' sugar*, divided
2 tablespoons sugar
Pearlized luster spray, such as Pearl Color Mist Food
    Color Spray (*wilton.com*)
1 recipe Apricot-Mascarpone Filling (recipe follows)

• Place egg whites in a medium bowl, and let sit at
room temperature, uncovered, for exactly 3 hours.
(Aging egg whites in this manner is essential to
creating perfect French macarons.)
• Line several baking sheets with parchment paper.
Using a pencil, draw 1½-inch circles 2 inches apart on
parchment paper. Turn parchment paper over. Set aside.
• In the workbowl of a food processor, combine
macadamia nuts and 1 tablespoon confectioners'
sugar, pulsing until finely ground. (Don't overprocess
or a nut butter will be created. The nut particles should
stay separate and dry but not clump together.) Add
remaining confectioners' sugar, and process just until
combined. Set aside.
• Beat egg whites at medium-high speed with an
electric mixer until frothy. Gradually add sugar, beating
at high speed until stiff peaks form, 3 to 5 minutes.
(Egg whites should be thick, creamy, and shiny.)
• Add macadamia mixture to egg whites, folding
gently by hand until well combined. Let batter sit
for 15 minutes.
• Transfer batter to a pastry bag fitted with a medium
round tip (Wilton #12). Pipe batter into drawn circles
on prepared baking sheets.
• Slam pans vigorously on the counter 5 to 7 times to
release air bubbles.
• Let sit at room temperature for 45 to 60 minutes
before baking to help develop the macaron's signature
crisp exterior when baked. (Macarons should feel dry
to the touch and should not stick to finger.)
• Preheat oven to 275°.
• Bake until firm to the touch, approximately 20 minutes.
Let cool completely on pans, then remove to airtight
containers. Refrigerate until ready to fill and serve.
• If desired, spray tops of macarons with pearlized
luster spray. Let dry.
• Place Apricot-Mascarpone Filling in a pastry bag
fitted with a medium round tip (Wilton #12). Pipe filling onto flat side of a macaron, and top with another
macaron, flat sides together, pushing down lightly

and twisting so filling spreads to edges. Repeat with
remaining macarons and filling.
• Serve immediately, or refrigerate in an airtight container for up to 3 days. Let come to room temperature
before serving.

**To measure confectioners' sugar accurately, spoon
lightly into measuring cup, and level off with a straight
edge. Do not pack or scoop sugar into cup as this will
negatively affect final product.*

Apricot-Mascarpone Filling

Yield: 1 cup
Preparation: 20 minutes

½ cup dried apricot halves
2 cups boiling water
1 (8-ounce) container mascarpone cheese
2 teaspoons heavy whipping cream
Peach food coloring paste, such as Wilton Creamy Peach

• Place apricot halves in a heatproof bowl, and cover
with boiling water. Let stand for 15 minutes to hydrate.
Drain well.
• Place apricots in the work bowl of a food processor,
and process until very finely chopped.
• In a small bowl, combine chopped apricots, mascarpone cheese, and cream, stirring until smooth and
creamy. If desired, tint mixture with food coloring paste.

"There are few hours in life more agreeable than the hour dedicated to the ceremony known as afternoon tea."

—Henry James

Mini Pound Cakes

Yield: 19 mini cakes
Preparation: 35 minutes
Bake: 10 minutes

3 large eggs, at room temperature
3 tablespoons whole milk, at room temperature
1 teaspoon vanilla extract
1½ cups cake flour
¾ cup sugar
1 teaspoon baking powder
¼ teaspoon salt
¾ cup butter, softened
4 ounces cream cheese, softened
1 recipe White Chocolate Ganache (recipe follows)
Garnish: fresh violas

• Preheat oven to 350°.
• Spray 19 wells of 2 (12-well) brownie pans* with non-stick cooking spray with flour. Set aside.
• In a small bowl, combine eggs, milk, and vanilla extract, whisking until blended. Set aside.
• In a large bowl, combine flour, sugar, baking powder, and salt, whisking well. Add butter, cream cheese, and half of egg mixture. Beat at low speed with an electric mixer just until dry ingredients are moistened. Increase mixer speed to medium, and beat for 1 minute. Using a rubber spatula, scrape down sides of bowl. Gradually add remaining egg mixture in 2 parts, beating for 30 seconds after each addition.
• Using a levered 3-tablespoon scoop, drop batter into prepared wells of pans. Spread surfaces smooth. Tap pans firmly several times on counter to remove air bubbles.
• Bake until a wooden pick inserted in the centers of cakes comes out clean, approximately 10 minutes. Let cool for 5 minutes. Remove from pans, invert onto wire racks, and let cool completely, bottom sides up.
• When cakes are cool, turn over, and trim any rounded cake tops, if necessary, so that cakes are level.
• Working carefully but quickly, spoon White Chocolate Ganache over cakes while still on wire racks, letting excess ganache drip off cakes. Let ganache set.
• Garnish each cake with a fresh viola, if desired.
• Refrigerate cakes in an airtight container for up to a day. Let come to room temperature before serving.

We used Pampered Chef brownie pans, available at pamperedchef.com.

MAKE-AHEAD TIP: *Cakes may be made ahead and frozen, unglazed, in airtight containers for up to 1 week. Let thaw, then glaze and garnish before serving.*

White Chocolate Ganache

Yield: 2 cups
Preparation: 10 minutes

3 (4-ounce) bars white chocolate, such as Ghirardelli
1 cup heavy whipping cream

• Place chocolate in a microwave-safe bowl. Melt chocolate in the microwave, according to package directions.
• In a small saucepan, scald cream, and slowly add to melted chocolate, stirring until smooth and creamy. Use immediately.

Peanut Butter Mousse in Dark Chocolate Cups

Yield: 12 servings
Preparation: 20 minutes

½ cup peanut butter morsels
½ cup plus 2 tablespoons heavy whipping cream, divided
2 tablespoons creamy peanut butter
½ teaspoon vanilla extract
2 tablespoons confectioners' sugar
12 dark chocolate tasting/cordial cups, such as Dobla
Garnish: grated dark chocolate

• In a medium microwave-safe bowl, combine peanut butter morsels and 2 tablespoons cream. Microwave at 50 percent power in 15-second intervals until melted, approximately 1½ minutes. Stir until smooth and creamy. Add peanut butter, and stir until combined. Let cool slightly.
• In a mixing bowl, combine remaining ½ cup cream and vanilla extract. Beat at high speed with an electric mixer until thick and creamy, stopping just before stiff peaks form. Add cooled peanut-butter mixture, whisking until incorporated.
• Transfer mixture to a piping bag fitted with a small closed-star tip (Wilton #21). Pipe into dark chocolate cups. Serve immediately, or refrigerate for up to 2 hours, and let come to room temperature before serving.
• Garnish with grated dark chocolate, if desired.

EDITOR'S NOTE

For tips on using fresh flowers
for garnish, see page 105.

SCONE

Pink Peppercorn–Rose Scones

🍵 *Capital Teas' Royal Wedding Tea*

SAVORIES

Parmesan-Chive Gougères

Tarragon–Poppy Seed Chicken Salad in Flower Cups

Cucumber-Cheese Canapés

🍵 *Dong Ding Oolong Tea*

SWEETS

Mango-Coconut Cream Tartlets

Lavender Madeleines

Lemon Buttercream Cakes

🍵 *Darjeeling First Flush Black Tea*

Mother's DAY

KITCHEN *Tip*

To crush pink pepper-
corns, place whole pep-
percorns in a heavy-duty,
resealable plastic bag,
and tap with a rolling
pin or a meat mallet.

Pink Peppercorn–Rose Scones

Yield: 12 scones
Preparation: 25 minutes
Bake: 18 minutes

1¾ cups all-purpose flour
2 teaspoons baking powder
1½ teaspoons crushed pink peppercorns
½ teaspoon salt
4 tablespoons cold unsalted butter, cut into pieces
¾ cup plus 2 tablespoons cold heavy whipping cream
½ teaspoon rose water, such as Nielson-Massey
1 recipe Pink Glaze (recipe follows)
Garnish: ground pink peppercorns

- Preheat oven to 350°.
- Line a rimmed baking sheet with parchment paper. Set aside.
- In a large bowl, combine flour, baking powder, peppercorns, and salt, whisking until blended. Using a pastry blender, cut butter into flour mixture until mixture resembles coarse crumbs.
- In a measuring cup, combine cream and rose water. Add cream mixture to flour mixture, stirring until a crumbly dough forms. Bring dough together with hands to form a ball. (If dough seems dry and won't come together, add more cream, 1 tablespoon at a time, until uniformly moist.)
- On a lightly floured surface, turn out dough, and knead 3 to 4 times. Using a rolling pin, roll out dough to a ½-inch thickness. Using a 2½-inch flower-shaped cutter, cut 12 shapes from dough, rerolling scraps as necessary. Place scones 2 inches apart on prepared baking sheet.
- Bake until edges of scones are golden brown and a wooden pick inserted in the centers comes out clean, approximately 18 minutes. Remove scones from baking sheet, and let cool completely on a wire rack.
- Spread Pink Glaze on tops of scones.
- Garnish with ground pink peppercorns, if desired.

Pink Glaze

Yield: ½ cup
Preparation: 5 minutes

1½ cups confectioners' sugar
2 tablespoons whole milk
Pink paste food coloring, such as Wilton

- In a small bowl, combine confectioners' sugar and milk, whisking until smooth and creamy. Add food coloring until glaze reaches desired shade of pink.
- Use immediately.

Parmesan-Chive Gougères

Yield: 31 gougères
Preparation: 30 minutes
Bake: 20 minutes

½ cup water
½ cup whole milk
½ cup butter
¼ teaspoon salt
1 cup all-purpose flour
4 large eggs
1 cup finely grated Parmesan cheese
1 tablespoon minced fresh chives
¼ teaspoon ground black pepper
Garnish: additional finely grated Parmesan cheese

- Preheat oven to 400°.
- Line 2 baking sheets with parchment paper. Set aside.
- In a medium saucepan, combine water, milk, butter, and salt; bring to a boil over medium-high heat. Reduce heat to low. Add flour, stirring with a wooden spoon until a smooth dough forms, approximately 2 minutes. Turn dough out into a large bowl. Let cool for 1 minute.
- Add eggs to dough, one at a time, beating at medium speed with an electric mixer until thoroughly incorporated. Add cheese, chives, and pepper, beating just until incorporated.
- Transfer dough to a pastry bag fitted with a large open-star tip (Wilton #1M). Pipe 1¼-inch rosettes 2 inches apart onto prepared baking sheets.
- Garnish with additional cheese, if desired.
- Bake until puffed and golden brown, 20 to 22 minutes.
- Serve warm.

MAKE-AHEAD TIP: *Gougères can be be baked 1 week in advance and frozen in an airtight container. To serve, place on a rimmed baking sheet, and heat in a 350° oven until warm, 3 to 5 minutes.*

Refrigerate in a covered container until cold, at least 4 hours. (Chicken salad may be made a day in advance and refrigerated until needed.)
• Arrange watercress in bottom of Toasted Wheat Flower Cups. Place scoops of chicken salad on top of watercress.
• Garnish with chopped almonds, if desired.

Toasted Wheat Flower Cups

Yield: 8 cups
Preparation: 15 minutes
Bake: 17 minutes

8 slices wheat bread, such as Pepperidge Farm
    Farmhouse 100% Whole Wheat
2 tablespoons melted butter

• Preheat oven to 350°.
• Using a rolling pin, roll bread slices until thin to make flexible. Using a 4-inch flower-shaped cutter, cut 8 shapes from bread. Press bread shapes into 8 wells of a 12-well whoopee pie pan, and brush surfaces with melted butter.
• Bake until crisp, approximately 17 minutes. Remove from pan, and let bread cups cool completely on a wire rack.
• Store in an airtight container until needed. (For optimum freshness, we recommend making bread cups the same day you plan to use them.)

Tarragon–Poppy Seed Chicken Salad in Flower Cups

Yield: 8 servings
Preparation: 15 minutes
Refrigerate: 4 hours

½ cup mayonnaise
1 tablespoon rice vinegar
1 teaspoon poppy seeds
¼ teaspoon salt
⅛ teaspoon ground black pepper
2 cups chopped roasted chicken
½ cup chopped green grapes
⅓ cup chopped toasted slivered almonds
1 tablespoon minced fresh tarragon
¼ cup watercress
1 recipe Toasted Wheat Flower Cups (recipe follows)
Garnish: finely chopped almonds

• In a medium bowl, combine mayonnaise, rice vinegar, poppy seeds, salt, and pepper, whisking well. Set aside.
• In the work bowl of a food processor, pulse chicken until finely chopped. Add chicken, grapes, almonds and tarragon to mayonnaise mixture, stirring to combine.

Cucumber-Cheese Canapés

Yield: 24 canapés
Preparation: 25 minutes

8 slices thin white sandwich bread, such as
    Pepperidge Farm Very Thin White
1 (5.2-ounce) container garlic and herb soft cheese,
    such as Boursin, at room temperature
24 very thin slices English cucumber

• Using a 1½-inch round cutter, cut 24 rounds from bread slices.
• Place cheese in a piping bag fitted with a medium open-star tip (Wilton #32). Pipe a rosette of cheese onto each bread round. Top each with a slice of cucumber, pressing down to spread cheese outward.
• Pipe a decorative rosette on top of cucumber slices.
• Serve immediately.

MAKE-AHEAD TIP: *Sandwiches can be covered with damp papers towels, and placed in an airtight container in the refrigerator until serving time.*

Mango–Coconut Cream Tartlets

Yield: 6 tartlets
Preparation: 45 minutes
Refrigerate: 4 hours

⅓ cup sugar
2 tablespoons all-purpose flour
¼ teaspoon salt
1¼ cups canned coconut milk*
¼ teaspoon coconut extract
1 (20-ounce) jar fresh mango slices, such as
   Del Monte Sun Fresh
6 (3.15-inch) shortbread tart shells, such as
   Clearbrook Farms
Garnish: fresh mint

• In a small saucepan, combine sugar, flour, salt, and coconut milk, whisking well. Cook over medium heat until mixture comes to a boil and thickens. (Whisk constantly, and reduce heat if filling begins to scorch.) Remove from heat, and add coconut extract, whisking to blend. Pour filling into a bowl, cover surface with plastic wrap, and refrigerate until cold, approximately 4 hours.
• Using a sharp paring knife, cut mango slices into very thin vertical slices, reserving syrup from jar. Set aside.
• Spoon cold coconut cream filling into tart shells. Arrange mango slices in concentric circles atop filling, using varying lengths, to resemble a rose. Brush with reserved mango syrup. (See step-by-step How-tos on page 128.)
• Garnish with fresh mint, if desired.

*Whisk canned coconut milk before using to blend the solids and liquid in the can.

MAKE-AHEAD TIP: *Coconut filling can be made a day in advance and refrigerated until needed. Two hours before serving, assemble tartlets, cover lightly with plastic wrap, and refrigerate until serving time.*

Lavender Madeleines

Yield: 36 madeleines
Preparation: 2½ hours
Bake: 7 minutes

4 large eggs
¾ cup sugar
1½ teaspoons vanilla extract
1 cup all-purpose flour
1 teaspoon baking powder
⅛ teaspoon salt
2 teaspoons culinary lavender, such as McCormick
½ cup butter, melted and cooled
1 recipe Confectioners' Sugar Glaze (recipe follows)

• Preheat oven to 350°.
• Spray wells of 3 (12-well) madeleine pans with non-stick cooking spray with flour. Set aside.
• In a large mixing bowl, combine eggs, sugar, and vanilla extract. Beat at high speed with an electric mixer until pale and fluffy, approximately 5 minutes. Set aside.
• In a small bowl, combine flour, baking powder, salt, and lavender, whisking well. Add half of flour mixture to egg mixture, beating at medium speed until incorporated. Add remaining flour mixture. Gradually add melted butter, beating until well blended. Let mixture stand for 5 minutes. Spoon 1 tablespoon batter into each well of prepared pans.
• Bake until lightly golden, 7 to 8 minutes. Remove madeleines from pans, and let cool completely on wire racks.
• Spoon Confectioners' Sugar Glaze over madeleines, and let dry, approximately 2 hours.
• Store in an airtight container.

Confectioners' Sugar Glaze

Yield: 1⅓ cups
Preparation: 5 minutes

3 cups confectioners' sugar
¼ cup plus 2 tablespoons whole milk
Lavender paste food coloring, such as Wilton violet

• In a medium bowl, combine confectioners' sugar and milk, whisking until smooth and creamy. Add more milk, a few drops at a time, until desired consistency is reached. Add lavender food coloring until desired color is reached.
• Use immediately.

Lemon Buttercream Cakes

Yield: 12 cakes
Preparation: 45 minutes
Bake: 20 minutes

1 (18.25-ounce) lemon cake mix, such as
    Duncan Hines Lemon Supreme
3 large eggs
1 cup water
¼ cup vegetable oil
⅓ cup sour cream
1 recipe Lemon Buttercream (recipe follows)
Garnish: fresh primroses

• Preheat oven to 350°.
• Line a 17-x-11-inch rimmed baking sheet with parchment paper. Spray with nonstick cooking spray. Set aside.
• In a large bowl, combine cake mix, eggs, water, oil, and sour cream. Beat at low speed with an electric mixer until moistened, approximately 30 seconds. Increase speed to medium, and beat for 2 minutes, scraping sides of bowl as necessary. Pour batter into prepared pan, and level with a spatula. Rap pan on the countertop sharply several times to reduce air bubbles.
• Bake until cake is golden brown and a wooden pick inserted in the center comes out clean, 18 to 20 minutes. Let cake cool completely in pan.
• When cake has cooled, cut 24 rounds from cake, using a 2¼-inch round cutter.
• Place Lemon Buttercream in a piping bag fitted with a large open-star tip (Wilton #1M). Pipe a circle of buttercream onto 12 cake rounds. Top each with another round of cake, pressing lightly to adhere. Pipe a decorative rosette of buttercream onto top of each cake round.
• Garnish each cake with a fresh primrose, if desired.

MAKE-AHEAD TIP: *Cake may be baked in advance, cut into rounds, and frozen in an airtight container, with layers separated by waxed paper, for up to a week. Let come to room temperature before frosting. Store, covered, in the refrigerator until ready to serve.*

Lemon Buttercream

Yield: 3½ cups
Preparation: 5 minutes

1 cup salted butter, softened
6 cups confectioners' sugar
2 teaspoons fresh lemon zest
¼ cup fresh lemon juice
1½ teaspoons lemon extract
Yellow paste food coloring, such as Wilton
    lemon yellow

• In a large bowl, combine butter, confectioners' sugar, lemon zest, lemon juice, and lemon extract. Beat at low speed with an electric mixer until combined, scraping down sides of bowl as necessary. Increase speed to high, and beat until light and fluffy. Add food coloring until desired shade of yellow is achieved.
• Use immediately, or refrigerate in an airtight container until needed. Let buttercream come to room temperature before using, and beat at high speed with an electric mixer for 1 minute.

MENU

SCONE

Pineapple-Coconut Scones
Harney & Sons' Tropical Green Tea

SAVORIES

Curried Smoked Turkey Salad Sandwiches
Lemon-Artichoke Crostini
Mini Broccoli Quiches
Teas Etc's Meyer Lemon Black Tea

SWEETS

Blueberry Cream Tartlets with Maple Glaze
Basil-Lime Sugar Cookies
Strawberry Ruffle Cakes
Golden Monkey Black Tea

Birthday

"Scones. The mere mention of this baked good conjures up memories of times well spent enjoying afternoon tea."

—Lorna Reeves

Pineapple-Coconut Scones

Yield: 14 scones
Preparation: 15 minutes
Bake: 18 to 20 minutes

2 cups all-purpose flour
2 tablespoons sugar
2 teaspoons baking powder
½ teaspoon salt
4 tablespoons cold salted butter, cut into pieces
½ cup crushed pineapple, drained
⅓ cup minced toasted sweetened flaked coconut
1 cup plus 1 tablespoon cold heavy whipping cream, divided
½ teaspoon vanilla extract
Lemon curd (optional)
Devon cream (optional)

• Preheat oven to 350°.
• Line a rimmed baking sheet with parchment paper. Set aside.
• In a large bowl, combine flour, sugar, baking powder, and salt, whisking well. Using a pastry blender, cut butter into flour mixture until mixture resembles coarse crumbs. Add pineapple and coconut, stirring to combine. Set aside.
• In a measuring cup, combine 1 cup cream and vanilla extract. Add cream to flour mixture, stirring until a dough forms. (If mixture seems dry, add more cream, 1 tablespoon at a time, until uniformly moist.)
• Turn dough out onto a lightly floured surface, and knead lightly 3 to 4 times. Using a rolling pin, roll dough to a ½-inch thickness. Using a 2¼-inch round cutter, cut 14 rounds from dough, rerolling scraps as necessary. Place scones 2 inches apart on prepared baking sheet.
• Brush tops of scones with remaining 1 tablespoon cream.
• Bake until edges of scones are golden brown and a wooden pick inserted in the centers comes out clean, 18 to 20 minutes.
• Serve with lemon curd and Devon cream, if desired.

KITCHEN *Tip*

When cutting out shapes from whole bread slices for tea sandwiches, freeze the scraps to make bread crumbs later.

Curried Smoked Turkey Salad Sandwiches

Yield: 8 tea sandwiches
Preparation: 25 minutes
Refrigerate: 4 hours

2 cups sliced smoked turkey*
½ cup mayonnaise
2 tablespoons fresh lime juice
1 teaspoon curry powder
¼ teaspoon ground black pepper
½ cup golden raisins
¼ cup finely chopped red bell pepper
¼ cup finely chopped celery
¼ cup chopped toasted almonds
1 tablespoon chopped fresh parsley
16 slices white sandwich bread, such as
   Pepperidge Farm
8 leaves butter lettuce

• Place turkey in the work bowl of a food processor, and process until finely ground.
• In a medium bowl, combine mayonnaise, lime juice, curry powder, and black pepper, whisking to blend. Add turkey, raisins, bell pepper, celery, almonds, and parsley, stirring until combined. Add more mayonnaise, if needed, to achieve desired consistency. Place in a covered container, and refrigerate until cold, approximately 4 hours.
• Using a 2½-inch round cutter, cut 16 rounds from bread slices.
• Place a lettuce leaf on each of 8 bread rounds. Top lettuce evenly with turkey salad. Top with remaining bread slices. Secure with a decorative pick, if desired.

*Chopped roasted chicken, pulled from a deli rotisserie chicken, can be substituted for smoked turkey.

MAKE-AHEAD TIP: *Make turkey salad a day in advance to allow time for flavors to meld and mellow. Assemble sandwiches 1 hour in advance, cover with damp paper towels, and place in an airtight container in the refrigerator until needed.*

Lemon-Artichoke Crostini

Yield: 24 crostini
Preparation: 20 minutes
Bake: 5 minutes

24 (¼-inch) slices French baguette
1 tablespoon butter, melted
4 ounces cream cheese, softened
½ cup chopped marinated artichokes
1 teaspoon fresh lemon zest, divided
1 teaspoon fresh lemon juice

½ teaspoon fresh thyme leaves
Garnish: fresh thyme sprigs

• Preheat oven to 350°.
• Line a rimmed baking sheet with parchment paper.
• Place baguette slices on prepared baking sheet, and brush lightly with melted butter.
• Bake until light golden brown, approximately 5 minutes. Remove from pan, and let cool.
• In a small bowl, combine cream cheese, artichokes, ½ teaspoon lemon zest, lemon juice, and thyme leaves, stirring until well blended. Divide cream cheese mixture evenly among baguette slices, spreading to cover.
• Garnish with remaining ½ teaspoon lemon zest and thyme sprigs, if desired.
• Serve immediately.

Mini Broccoli Quiches

Yield: 12 mini quiches
Preparation: 25 minutes
Refrigerate: 30 minutes
Bake: 12 minutes

1 (14.1-ounce) package refrigerated pie dough (2 sheets)
1 large egg
⅓ cup heavy whipping cream
¼ teaspoon salt
⅛ teaspoon ground black pepper
¼ cup finely shredded sharp white Cheddar cheese
½ cup cooked fresh broccoli florets, finely chopped

• Preheat oven to 450°.
• On a lightly floured surface, unroll both sheets of pie dough. Using a 2½-inch square cutter, cut 12 squares from pie dough. Press squares into the wells of a 12-well square mini cheesecake pan, trimming excess dough from edges. Refrigerate for 30 minutes.
• Prick bottoms of dough with a fork to prevent puffing during baking.
• Bake until light golden brown, approximately 5 minutes.
• In a liquid measuring cup, combine egg, cream, salt, and pepper, whisking well. Set aside.
• Divide cheese evenly among baked shells. Repeat with broccoli and then with egg mixture.
• Bake until mixture is slightly puffed, approximately 12 minutes. Let cool in pan for 5 minutes. Remove from pan, and let cool completely. Serve warm or at room temperature.

MAKE-AHEAD TIP: *Quiches may be made a day in advance and stored in a covered container in the refrigerator. Reheat on a rimmed baking sheet in a 350° oven until warm, approximately 5 minutes.*

Basil-Lime Sugar Cookies

Yield: 48 cookies
Preparation: 45 minutes
Bake: 8 minutes
Refrigerate: 1 hour 15 minutes
Dry: 1 hour

1½ cups all-purpose flour
½ teaspoon baking soda
¼ teaspoon salt
½ cup salted butter, softened
½ cup sugar
1 large egg
¼ teaspoon lemon extract
2 tablespoons finely chopped fresh basil
1 tablespoon fresh lime zest
2 tablespoons fresh lime juice
1 cup confectioners' sugar

• Line 2 baking sheets with parchment paper. Set aside.
• In a small bowl, combine flour, baking soda, and salt, whisking well. Set aside.
• In a large bowl, combine butter and sugar. Beat at medium speed with an electric mixer until light and creamy, approximately 2 minutes. Add egg and lemon extract, then basil and lime zest, beating to combine. Add flour mixture to butter mixture, beating until incorporated. Wrap dough in plastic wrap, and refrigerate until cold, approximately 1 hour.
• Preheat oven to 350°.
• On a lightly floured surface, roll dough to a ⅛-inch thickness. Using a 2-inch teapot-shaped cookie cutter, cut 48 shapes from dough, rerolling dough as necessary. (If dough becomes too warm to work with, refrigerate until firm.) Place cookies 2 inches apart on prepared baking sheets. Refrigerate for 15 minutes to prevent cookies from spreading and losing their shape.
• Bake until edges of cookies are light golden brown, approximately 8 minutes. Remove cookies to a wire rack, and let cool completely.
• In a small bowl, combine confectioners' sugar and lime juice, stirring until smooth and creamy. Add more lime juice, if necessary, to achieve desired consistency. Spread glaze over cookies using an offset spatula, and let dry for 1 hour.
• Store cookies in an airtight container between layers of waxed paper.

MAKE-AHEAD TIP: *Freeze unglazed cookies in an airtight container for up to a week. Thaw cookies, and then glaze.*

Blueberry Cream Tartlets with Maple Glaze

Yield: 8 tartlets
Preparation: 30 minutes
Refrigerate: 4 hours

1 (3-ounce) package cream cheese, softened
¼ cup plus 2 tablespoons sour cream
¼ cup plus 2 tablespoons light brown sugar
2 cups fresh blueberries
½ cup pure maple syrup
8 (3.15-inch) tart shells, such as Clearbrook Farms

• In a small bowl, combine cream cheese, sour cream, and brown sugar, beating at low speed with an electric mixer until smooth and creamy. Divide mixture evenly among tart shells. Arrange blueberries on top of cream-cheese filling. Cover, and refrigerate for up to 4 hours.
• In a small saucepan, reduce maple syrup by boiling gently until thick, approximately 3 minutes. Let cool slightly. Spoon over blueberries.
• Serve immediately.

Strawberry Ruffle Cakes

Yield: 12 mini cakes
Preparation: 1 hour
Bake: 15 minutes

2 cups cake flour
1 teaspoon baking powder
½ teaspoon salt
¼ teaspoon baking soda
½ cup salted butter, softened
1¼ cups sugar
½ cup seedless strawberry jam
3 large eggs
½ teaspoon vanilla extract
Red paste food coloring, such as Wilton No Taste Red
⅓ cup whole buttermilk
1 recipe Strawberry Buttercream (recipe follows)
Garnish: crystallized flowers*

• Preheat oven to 350°.
• Line a 17-x-12-inch rimmed baking sheet with parch-ment paper. Spray with nonstick cooking spray. Set aside.
• In a medium bowl, combine flour, baking powder, salt, and baking soda, whisking well. Set aside.
• In a large bowl, combine butter and sugar. Beat at high speed with an electric mixer until light and fluffy, approximately 4 minutes. Add jam, then eggs, one at a time, beating well after each addition. Scrape down sides of bowl, and add vanilla extract and enough food coloring to achieve desired shade of pink. Add flour mixture to butter mixture in thirds, alternately with but-termilk, beginning and ending with flour mixture. Beat at low speed until ingredients are combined. Spread batter evenly into prepared pan. Rap pan several times on countertop to reduce air bubbles in batter.
• Bake cake on middle rack of oven until a wooden pick inserted in the center comes out clean, approximately 15 minutes. Let cake cool completely in pan on a wire rack.
• Cut 3 (9-inch) cardboard cake rounds into quarters. Set aside.
• Using a 2¼-inch round cutter, cut 24 rounds from cooled cake. Place 1 cake round on a cardboard quarter, and spread 1 teaspoon Strawberry Buttercream on top. Top with another cake round, pressing cakes together. Repeat with remaining cake rounds and cardboard quar-ters. (See step-by-step How-to on page 129.)
• Place remaining buttercream in a piping bag fitted with a small petal tip (Ateco #101). With wider end of tip toward bottom, pipe vertical rows of ruffles around sides of cakes, starting at bottom and working upward. Pipe concentric ruffles on top of cake. Freeze cakes on cardboard quarters in an airtight container for up to a week. (Cakes will be easier to work with when frozen.)

• To serve, slide a thin spatula beneath frozen cakes to separate them from cardboard quarters, and place cakes on paper doilies on individual cake stands or serving plates. Let come to room temperature.
• Garnish with crystallized flowers, if desired.

We used Sweetfields brand crystallized flowers, available at sweetfields.com.

Strawberry Buttercream

Yield: 5 cups
Preparation: 5 minutes

1¼ cups salted butter, softened
7 cups confectioners' sugar
2¾ teaspoons strawberry extract
¼ cup plus 2 tablespoons whole milk

• In a large bowl, combine butter, sugar, strawberry extract, and milk. Beat at low speed with an electric mixer, gradually increasing to high speed, until mixture is smooth and fluffy. Scrape down sides of bowl as necessary.
• Use immediately or refrigerate in a covered container until needed. Let buttercream come to room tempera-ture before using. Beat with an electric mixer for 1 minute before using.

SCONE
Stollen Scones with Orange Curd
Nepal Ilam Black Tea

SAVORIES
Brie Cups with Red Pepper Glaze
Cranberry-Duck-Pecan Tea Sandwiches
Florentine Quiches
Darjeeling Pouchong Arya Green Tea

SWEETS
White Chocolate Cake
Apricot-Almond Snowballs
Chocolate-Hazelnut Thumbprint Cookies
Simpson & Vail's Almond Sugar Cookie Black Tea

Christmas

Stollen Scones

Yield: 15 scones
Preparation: 25 minutes
Bake: 20 minutes

2 cups all-purpose flour
⅓ cup sugar
2 teaspoons baking powder
1 teaspoon fresh lemon zest
½ teaspoon salt
½ teaspoon ground allspice
½ teaspoon ground cinnamon
¼ cup cold salted butter, cut into pieces
⅓ cup chopped mixed candied fruits
⅓ cup golden raisins
⅓ cup toasted chopped almonds
¾ cup plus 2 tablespoons cold heavy
    whipping cream
½ teaspoon almond extract
Garnish: confectioners' sugar
Orange Curd (recipe follows)
Devon cream (optional)

• Preheat oven to 350°.
• Line a rimmed baking sheet with parchment paper. Set aside.
• In a large bowl, combine flour, sugar, baking powder, lemon zest, salt, allspice, and cinnamon, whisking well. Using a pastry blender, cut butter into flour mixture until mixture resembles coarse crumbs. Add candied fruits, raisins, and almonds, stirring well. Set aside.
• In a measuring cup, combine cream and almond extract, stirring well. Add cream mixture to flour mixture, stirring until a soft dough forms. (If mixture seems dry and won't come together, add more cream, 1 tablespoon at a time, until dough is uniformly moist).
• Using a levered 3-tablespoon scoop, drop dough 2 inches apart onto prepared baking sheet.
• Bake until edges of scones are golden brown and a wooden pick inserted in the centers comes out clean, approximately 20 minutes. Transfer scones to a wire rack, and let cool slightly.
• Dust with confectioners' sugar, if desired.
• Serve with Orange Curd and Devon cream, if desired.

Orange Curd

Yield: ¾ cup
Preparation: 15 minutes
Cook: 3 minutes
Refrigerate: 4 hours

¼ cup butter
4 large egg yolks
½ cup fresh orange juice
⅓ cup sugar
1 tablespoon fresh orange zest

• In a medium saucepan, melt butter over low heat. Remove from heat. Let cool slightly.
• In a medium bowl, combine egg yolks, orange juice, and sugar, whisking well. Gradually add melted butter to egg yolk mixture, whisking constantly. Return to saucepan. Cook over medium heat, stirring constantly, until mixture coats the back of a spoon, 2 to 3 minutes. Reduce heat to prevent mixture from boiling, if necessary.
• Strain curd through a fine-mesh sieve, discarding solids. Add orange zest to curd, stirring well.
• Refrigerate in an airtight container until cold and thickened, at least 4 hours and up to 3 days.

Brie Cups with Red Pepper Glaze

Yield: 15 servings
Preparation: 15 minutes
Bake: 5 minutes

1 (1.9-ounce) package mini phyllo cups, such as Athens
⅓ cup Brie cheese (approximately 6 ounces),
    cut into cubes
3 tablespoons red pepper jelly
Garnish: fresh thyme sprigs

• Preheat oven to 350°.
• Line a rimmed baking sheet with parchment paper.
• Arrange phyllo cups on prepared pan. Place a cube of Brie in each cup.
• Bake until Brie melts, 5 to 7 minutes.
• Divide red pepper jelly evenly among phyllo cups, and spread over warm cheese.
• Garnish with fresh thyme sprigs, if desired.
• Serve immediately.

Cranberry-Duck-Pecan Tea Sandwiches

Yield: 20 sandwiches
Preparation: 25 minutes
Refrigerate: 4 hours

1 (8-ounce) package fully cooked rotisserie duck
    breasts, such as Maple Leaf Farms
¼ cup finely chopped dried cranberries
3 tablespoons finely chopped toasted pecans
3 tablespoons finely chopped celery
⅓ cup mayonnaise
1 teaspoon fresh orange zest
2 teaspoons fresh orange juice
20 slices white sandwich bread, such as Pepperidge
    Farm Farmhouse Style
Garnish: sliced fresh cranberries and fresh rosemary
    sprigs

• Heat duck according to package directions. Remove and discard skin. Rinse excess rotisserie seasonings from duck, and pat dry with paper towels.
• In the work bowl of a food processor, pulse duck until finely chopped.
• In a medium bowl, combine chopped duck, cranberries, pecans, celery, mayonnaise, orange zest, and orange juice, stirring to combine. Refrigerate in an airtight container until cold—at least 4 hours and up to a day.
• Using a 2-inch round cutter, cut 40 rounds from bread slices.
• Place approximately 1 tablespoon duck salad on each of 20 bread rounds. Top with remaining bread rounds.

• Garnish with fresh cranberry slices and rosemary sprigs, if desired.

MAKE-AHEAD TIP: *Sandwiches may be made earlier in the day (minus garnish), covered with damp paper towels, and refrigerated in an airtight container. Garnish just before serving.*

Florentine Quiches

Yield: 6 (4-inch) mini quiches
Preparation: 30 minutes
Refrigerate: 30 minutes
Bake: 25 minutes

1 (14.1-ounce) package refrigerated pie dough
    (2 sheets)
½ teaspoon olive oil
1 (6-ounce) package fresh baby spinach
⅓ cup heavy whipping cream
1 large egg
½ cup coarsely shredded fontina cheese
6 tablespoons freshly grated Parmesan cheese
36 grape tomato slices
¼ teaspoon garlic salt
¼ teaspoon Italian seasoning
⅛ teaspoon ground black pepper

• Preheat oven to 450°.
• Using a 4½-inch round cutter, cut 6 rounds from pie dough, and press into 4-inch tart pans, trimming edges to fit. Refrigerate for 30 minutes
• Place tart pans on a rimmed baking sheet. Prick bottoms of dough to prevent puffing during baking.
• Bake until light golden brown, approximately 8 minutes. Transfer tart pans to wire racks, and let cool completely.
• Reduce oven temperature to 350°.
• In a large nonstick sauté pan, heat olive oil over medium-high heat. Add spinach, stirring constantly, until wilted and tender. Transfer spinach to a small bowl, and let cool. Chop spinach finely, and squeeze to remove excess liquid. Set aside.
• In a small bowl, combine cream and egg, whisking well. Set aside.
• Return pans to rimmed baking sheet. Divide cheeses evenly among prepared tart pans. Top evenly with spinach and tomato slices. Sprinkle evenly with garlic salt, Italian seasoning, and pepper. Divide egg mixture among tart pans.
• Bake until filling is slightly puffed, approximately 25 minutes. (Filling will fall as it cools.)
• Serve within 3 hours, or cover and refrigerate. Reheat in a 350° oven until warm.

1 (4-ounce) white chocolate baking bar, such as
 Ghirardelli, melted
1 recipe White Chocolate Buttercream
 (recipe follows)
Garnish: fresh currants

• Preheat oven to 350°.
• Spray 2 (9-inch) round cake pans with nonstick baking
spray with flour. Set aside.
• In a large bowl, combine cake mix, eggs, water, oil,
and sour cream. Beat at low speed with an electric
mixer until moistened, approximately 30 seconds.
Increase speed to medium, and beat for 2 minutes,
scraping sides of bowl as necessary. Add melted white
chocolate, beating at low speed until incorporated.
Divide batter evenly between prepared pans.
• Bake until a wooden pick inserted near the centers of
cakes comes out clean, approximtely 25 minutes. Let
cakes cool in pans for 5 minutes. Remove from pans,
and let cool completely on wire racks.
• Using a long, sharp serrated knife, trim tops of cakes
so that rounds are completely level. Turn cakes over so
that cut sides are down.
• Using a long spatula, frost top and sides of each cake
with White Chocolate Buttercream, smoothing surface.
• Serve immediately, or refrigerate, covered, until serving time (no more than 24 hours).
• Using a long, sharp knife with a smooth cutting
edge, cut each cake into 16 equal wedges.
• Garnish with fresh currants, if desired.

White Chocolate Buttercream
Yield: 2¾ cups
Preparation: 5 minutes

¾ cup butter, softened
4 cups confectioners' sugar
¼ cup plus 3 tablespoons heavy whipping cream
½ teaspoon vanilla extract
¼ teaspoon salt
1 (4-ounce) white chocolate baking bar, such as
 Ghirardelli, melted

• In a large bowl, combine butter, confectioners' sugar,
cream, vanilla extract, and salt. Beat at low speed with
an electric mixer until combined. Increase speed to
high, and beat until fluffy and creamy. Add melted
white chocolate, beating until incorporated.
• Use immediately, or store in an airtight container in
the refrigerator for up to a day. (Let come to room temperature before using. Beat buttercream at medium
speed with an electric mixer for 1 minute before using.)

White Chocolate Cake
Yield: 32 servings
Preparation: 35 minutes
Bake: 25 minutes

1 (16.5-ounce) package white cake mix
3 large eggs
1 cup water
¼ cup vegetable oil
⅓ cup sour cream

Apricot-Almond Snowballs

Yield: 40 candies
Preparation: 30 minutes
Cook: 5 minutes
Refrigerate: 4 hours

1½ cups sweetened flaked coconut
¼ cup butter
⅓ cup sugar
1 large egg yolk
1 cup whole dried apricots, finely chopped
½ teaspoon vanilla extract
½ cup toasted, chopped, blanched almonds
1½ cups crispy puffed rice cereal

• Place coconut in the work bowl of a food processor. Pulse until finely chopped. Transfer to a small bowl, and set aside.
• In a medium saucepan, melt butter over low heat. Remove from heat. Add sugar and egg yolk, stirring to combine. Add apricots, and return pan to medium heat. Cook, stirring constantly, for 5 minutes. Remove pan from heat, and add vanilla extract, stirring to incorporate. Add almonds and rice cereal, stirring vigorously to incorporate.
• Using a levered 2-teaspoon scoop, drop candy mixture into coconut to coat. Roll into balls between palms of hands, pressing mixture together, if necessary, to hold shape.
• Refrigerate candies in an airtight container until cold, at least 4 hours.
• Serve immediately, or freeze for up to a week.

Chocolate-Hazelnut Thumbprint Cookies

Yield: 46 cookies
Preparation: 30 minutes
Bake: 15 minutes

1¾ cups all-purpose flour
½ cup finely ground hazelnuts
¼ teaspoon salt
1 cup salted butter, softened
⅔ cup sugar
2 large egg yolks
1 teaspoon vanilla extract
1 recipe Dark Chocolate Ganache Filling (recipe follows)
Garnish: finely chopped hazelnuts

• Preheat oven to 350°.
• Line 2 rimmed baking sheets with parchment paper. Set aside.
• In a small bowl, combine flour, hazelnuts, and salt, whisking well. Set aside.
• In a medium bowl, combine butter and sugar. Beat at high speed with an electric mixer until light and creamy. Add egg yolks and vanilla extract, beating until combined. Add flour mixture, beating until incorporated.
• Using a levered 2-teaspoon scoop, drop dough 2 inches apart onto prepared baking sheets. Using a finger or the back of a rounded measuring teaspoon, press an indentation into top of each cookie.
• Bake until edges of cookies are golden brown, approximately 15 minutes. (If indentations need reshaping, press with the back of a rounded measuring teaspoon.) Transfer cookies to a wire rack, and let cool completely.
• Fill each indentation with Dark Chocolate Ganache Filling.
• Garnish with chopped hazelnuts, if desired.

MAKE-AHEAD TIP: *Cookies can be made up to 3 days ahead and stored in an airtight container in the refrigerator or frozen for up to a week.*

Dark Chocolate Ganache Filling

Yield: approximately 2 cups
Preparation: 5 minutes
Cook: 5 minutes

¾ cup heavy whipping cream
1½ cups dark chocolate morsels

• In a small saucepan, scald cream over medium-high heat. Remove from heat, and add chocolate morsels. Let stand until morsels have melted, approximately 1 minute. Stir vigorously until smooth and creamy.
• Use immediately.

Create your own menu

Whether planning treats for two or a large crowd, putting together a menu for an afternoon tea can be challenging. One type of scone, three savory options, and three sweet offerings will fill most tiered stands with ease and are manageable to prepare. By following our tips for each of these categories, you can create teatime menus that are sure to please.

SCONES

Some hostesses and tearoom owners choose to serve scones as a first course because, as they point out, scones are best hot out of the oven. Others prefer scones as the second course, in which case they either place these breads on the corresponding tier of the stand to be eaten at room temperature or bring the warm scones to the table only at the appropriate time.

If scones are petite, allow two per person; otherwise, one each should be sufficient. Select a flavor and a shape that will be compatible with the other courses and with the selected theme. Choose condiments that complement the taste of the scone, and be sure to allow enough for each guest.

SAVORIES

Offer your guests three different options to enjoy for this course. While tea sandwiches are traditional favorites, consider incorporating savory tartlets, miniature quiches, and other flavorful bite-size items into the menu. Coordinate flavors, textures, and shapes with the tea-party theme. To avoid last-minute stress, opt for recipes that can be made ahead, at least in part, or that require minimum preparation time.

SWEETS

Because this course sits in the place of honor on the top tier of the stand and is the last to be eaten, incorporating a variety of shapes, flavors, textures, and colors here is quite important. Three sweets of different types will make the final installment of the tea menu interesting and memorable. Keep the portions small, especially if the treats are rich.

EMBELLISHMENTS

Fresh fruits and flowers can be colorful fillers for any tiered stand. Grapes, strawberries, raspberries, and orange wedges are popular choices. Star-fruit slices, kiwi slices, kumquats, and currants are less traditional but add wonderful shapes and flavors. Fruit slices that turn brown easily, such as apple and pear, should be tossed in citrus juice before using. Garnish trays with flowers that are pesticide free and food safe. Roses, pansies, marigolds, violas, primroses, and orchids are excellent choices. For more about garnishing with flowers, see page 105.

Scones

Cream Scones

Yield: 12 to 14 scones
Preparation: 20 minutes
Bake: 10 minutes

2 cups cake flour
2 tablespoons sugar
2½ teaspoons baking powder
½ teaspoon salt
4 tablespoons cold salted butter, cut into pieces
¾ cup plus 3 tablespoons cold heavy whipping cream, divided
Lemon curd (optional)
Devon cream (optional)

• Preheat oven to 400°.
• Line a rimmed baking sheet with parchment paper. Set aside.
• In a large bowl, combine flour, sugar, baking powder, and salt, whisking well. Using a pastry blender, cut butter into flour mixture until mixture resembles coarse crumbs. Add ¾ cup plus 2 tablespoons cream, stirring to combine. Bring mixture together with hands until a dough forms. Dough will be very stiff. (If mixture seems dry, add more cream, 1 tablespoon at a time, until uniformly moist.)
• Turn dough out onto a lightly floured surface. Knead lightly 3 to 4 times. Using a rolling pin, roll dough to a ½-inch thickness. Using a 2-inch scalloped-edge round cutter, cut rounds from dough, rerolling scraps as necessary. Place scones 2 inches apart on prepared baking sheet.
• Brush tops of scones with remaining 1 tablespoon cream.
• Bake until edges of scones are light golden brown and a wooden pick inserted in the centers comes out clean, approximately 10 minutes.
• Serve warm with lemon curd and Devon cream, if desired.

Currant-Spice Scones

Yield: 13 to 15 scones
Preparation: 20 minutes
Bake: 18 minutes

2 cups all-purpose flour
2 teaspoons baking powder
2 teaspoons ground ginger
1½ teaspoons ground cinnamon
½ teaspoon salt
¼ teaspoon ground mace
¼ teaspoon ground cloves
¼ teaspoon ground black pepper
¼ teaspoon ground nutmeg
4 tablespoons cold salted butter, cut into pieces
½ cup dried currants
¾ cup plus 3 tablespoons cold heavy whipping cream, divided
1 teaspoon vanilla extract
2 tablespoons turbinado sugar
Currant jam (optional)

• Preheat oven to 350°.
• Line a rimmed baking sheet with parchment paper. Set aside.
• In a large bowl, combine flour, baking powder, ginger, cinnamon, salt, mace, cloves, black pepper, and nutmeg, whisking well. Using a pastry blender, cut butter into flour mixture until mixture resembles coarse crumbs. Add currants, stirring to coat with flour mixture. Set aside.
• In a measuring cup, combine ¾ cup plus 2 table-spoons cream and vanilla extract, stirring to blend. Add cream mixture to flour mixture, stirring until crumbly. Bring mixture together with hands until a dough forms. (If mixture seems dry, add more cream, 1 tablespoon at a time, until uniformly moist.)
• Turn dough out onto a lightly floured surface. Knead lightly 3 to 4 times. Using a rolling pin, roll dough to a ½-inch thickness. Using a 3½-inch star-shaped cutter, cut shapes from dough, rerolling scraps as necessary. Place scones 2 inches apart on prepared baking sheet.
• Brush tops of scones with remaining 1 tablespoon cream. Sprinkle scones with turbinado sugar.
• Bake until edges of scones are golden brown and a wooden pick inserted in the centers comes out clean, approximately 18 minutes.
• Serve with currant jam, if desired.

Maple-Walnut Scones

Yield: 16 scones
Preparation: 20 minutes
Bake: 15 minutes

2 cups self-rising flour
⅓ cup sugar
4 tablespoons cold salted butter, cut into pieces
½ cup toasted chopped walnuts
1 cup cold heavy whipping cream
1 teaspoon maple flavoring
1 recipe Maple Glaze (recipe follows)
Garnish: fresh currants

• Preheat oven to 400°.
• Spray a 16-well mini scone pan* with nonstick cooking spray. Set aside.
• In a large bowl, combine flour and sugar, whisking well. Using a pastry blender, cut butter into flour mixture until mixture resembles coarse crumbs. Add walnuts, stirring to combine. Set aside.
• In a measuring cup, combine cream and maple flavoring, stirring to blend. Add cream mixture to flour mixture, stirring until a dough forms. (If mixture seems dry, add more cream, 1 tablespoon at a time, until uniformly moist.)
• Divide dough among wells of prepared pan, patting to create a level surface.
• Bake until edges of scones are golden brown and a wooden pick inserted in the centers comes out clean, approximately 15 minutes. Remove scones from pan, and let cool completely on a wire rack.
• Brush tops of scones with Maple Glaze.
• Garnish with currants, if desired.

We used a Nordicware Mini Scone Pan, which is available at nordicware.com.

Pear–Blue Cheese Scones

Yield: 15 to 17 scones
Preparation: 20 minutes
Bake: 20 minutes

2 cups all-purpose flour
⅓ cup sugar
2½ teaspoons baking powder
½ teaspoon salt
4 tablespoons cold salted butter, cut into pieces
1 cup chopped fresh pear
⅓ cup blue cheese crumbles
⅓ cup chopped toasted walnuts
¾ cup cold heavy whipping cream
½ teaspoon vanilla extract

• Preheat oven to 350°.
• Line 2 rimmed baking sheets with parchment paper. Set aside.
• In a large bowl, combine flour, sugar, baking powder, and salt, whisking well. Using a pastry blender, cut butter into flour mixture until mixture resembles coarse crumbs. Add pear, blue cheese, and walnuts, stirring until coated with flour mixture. Set aside.
• In a measuring cup, combine cream and vanilla extract, stirring to blend. Add cream mixture to flour mixture, stirring to incorporate. Mixture will still be crumbly. Bring mixture together with hands until a dough forms. (If mixture seems dry, add more cream, 1 tablespoon at a time, until uniformly moist.)
• Using a levered 3-tablespoon scoop, drop dough 2 inches apart onto prepared baking sheets.
• Bake until edges of scones are golden brown and a wooden pick inserted in the centers comes out clean, approximately 20 minutes.
• Serve warm.

Maple Glaze

Yield: 1 cup
Preparation: 5 minutes

1½ cups confectioners' sugar
¼ cup whole milk
⅛ teaspoon maple extract

• In a small bowl, combine confectioners' sugar, milk, and maple extract, whisking until smooth and creamy.
• Use immediately.

Apple-Caramel Drop Scones
Yield: 16 to 18 scones
Preparation: 20 minutes
Bake: 20 minutes

2 cups all-purpose flour
⅓ cup sugar
2¼ teaspoons baking powder
½ teaspoon salt
4 tablespoons cold salted butter, cut into pieces
1 cup chopped peeled apple, such as Golden Delicious
½ cup caramel bits, such as Kraft Premium
¾ cup plus 2 tablespoons cold heavy whipping cream
½ teaspoon vanilla extract
1 recipe Spiced Cream (recipe follows)

• Preheat oven to 350°.
• Line 2 rimmed baking sheets with parchment paper. Set aside.
• In a large bowl, combine flour, sugar, baking powder, and salt, whisking well. Using a pastry blender, cut butter into flour mixture until mixture resembles coarse crumbs. Add apple and caramel bits, stirring to combine. Set aside.
• In a measuring cup, combine cream and vanilla extract, stirring to blend. Add cream mixture to flour mixture, stirring until a dough forms. (If mixture seems dry, add more cream, 1 tablespoon at a time, until uniformly moist.)
• Using a levered 3-tablespoon scoop, drop dough 2 inches apart onto prepared baking sheets.
• Bake until edges of scones are golden brown and a wooden pick inserted in the centers comes out clean, approximately 20 minutes.
• Serve with Spiced Cream, if desired.

Spiced Cream
Yield: 2 cups
Preparation: 5 minutes

1 cup cold heavy whipping cream
3 tablespoons confectioners' sugar
½ teaspoon vanilla extract
¼ teaspoon ground cinnamon
⅛ teaspoon ground allspice

• In a mixing bowl, combine cream, confectioners' sugar, vanilla extract, cinnamon, and allspice. Beat at high speed with an electric mixer until stiff peaks form. Use immediately, or cover and refrigerate for up to a day.

Bacon, Goat Cheese, and Chive Scones
Yield: 12 to 14 scones
Preparation: 30 minutes
Bake: 12 minutes

2¼ cups self-rising flour
2 teaspoons sugar
4 tablespoons cold salted butter, cut into pieces
1 cup crumbled goat cheese
¼ cup chopped cooked bacon
2 tablespoons chopped fresh chives
1 cup plus 2 tablespoons cold heavy whipping cream, divided

• Preheat oven to 400°.
• Line a rimmed baking sheet with parchment paper. Set aside.
• In a large bowl, combine flour and sugar, whisking well. Using a pastry blender, cut butter into flour mixture until mixture resembles coarse crumbs. Add cheese, bacon, and chives, tossing until ingredients are coated with flour. Add 1 cup cream, stirring to combine. Bring mixture together with hands until a dough forms. (If mixture seems dry, add more cream, 1 tablespoon at a time, until uniformly moist.)
• Turn dough out onto a lightly floured surface. Knead lightly 3 to 4 times. Using a rolling pin, roll dough to a ½-inch thickness. Using a 2¼-inch square cutter, cut squares from dough, rerolling scraps as necessary. Place scones 2 inches apart on prepared baking sheet.
• Brush tops of scones with remaining 2 tablespoons cream.
• Bake until edges of scones are golden brown and a wooden pick inserted in the centers comes out clean, approximately 12 minutes.
• Serve warm.

(If mixture seems dry, add more coconut milk, 1 table-spoon at a time, until uniformly moist.)
• Turn dough out onto a lightly floured surface. Knead gently 3 to 4 times. Using a rolling pin, roll dough to ½-inch thickness. Using a 2½-inch round cutter, cut rounds from dough. Place scones 2 inches apart on prepared baking sheets.
• Bake until edges of scones are golden brown and a wooden pick inserted in the centers comes out clean, approximately 11 minutes.
• Serve warm.

Raspberries and Cream Scones

Yield: 21 to 23 scones
Preparation: 20 minutes
Bake: 19 minutes

1½ cups all-purpose flour
⅓ cup sugar
1½ teaspoons baking powder
¼ teaspoon salt
3 tablespoons cold salted butter, cut into pieces
¾ cup freeze-dried raspberries, such as Just Raspberries
1 (3-ounce) package cream cheese, cut into small cubes
¾ cup cold heavy whipping cream, divided
½ teaspoon vanilla extract

• Preheat oven to 350°.
• Line 2 rimmed baking sheets with parchment paper. Set aside.
• In a medium bowl, combine flour, sugar, baking pow-der, and salt, whisking well. Using a pastry blender, cut butter into flour mixture until mixture resembles coarse crumbs. Add raspberries and cubed cream cheese, tossing to coat with flour mixture. Set aside.
• In a measuring cup, combine ½ cup plus 2 table-spoons cream and vanilla extract, stirring to blend. Add cream mixture all at once to flour mixture, stirring to combine. Bring mixture together with hands until a stiff dough forms. (If mixture seems dry, add more cream, 1 tablespoon at a time, until uniformly moist.)
• Turn dough out onto a lightly floured surface. Knead gently 3 to 4 times. Using a rolling pin, roll dough to a ½-inch thickness. Using a 2-inch round cutter, cut rounds from dough, rerolling scraps as necessary. Place scones 2 inches apart on prepared baking sheets.
• Brush tops of scones with remaining 2 tablespoons cream.
• Bake until edges of scones are golden brown and a wooden pick inserted in the centers comes out clean, approximately 19 minutes.

Coconut, Lime, and Basil Scones

Yield: 13 to 15 scones
Preparation: 25 minutes
Bake: 11 minutes

3 cups self-rising flour
½ cup sugar
½ cup cold salted butter, cut into pieces
2 tablespoons minced fresh basil
4 teaspoons fresh lime zest
¾ cup plus 1 tablespoon canned coconut milk
2 teaspoons coconut extract

• Preheat oven to 400°.
• Line 2 rimmed baking sheets with parchment paper. Set aside.
• In a large bowl, combine flour and sugar, whisking well. Using a pastry blender, cut butter into flour mix-ture until mixture resembles coarse crumbs. Add basil and lime zest, stirring to incorporate. Set aside.
• In a measuring cup, combine coconut milk and coconut extract, whisking to blend. Add milk mixture to flour mixture, stirring until a dough forms. Bring mixture together with hands until a stiff dough forms.

Lemon-Macadamia Scones

Yield: 14 to 16 scones
Preparation: 25 minutes
Bake: 20 minutes

2 cups all-purpose flour
½ cup sugar
1 tablespoon fresh lemon zest
2 teaspoons baking powder
½ teaspoon salt
4 tablespoons cold salted butter, cut into pieces
⅓ cup chopped roasted, salted macadamia nuts
1¼ cups cold heavy whipping cream, divided
¼ teaspoon lemon extract

• Preheat oven to 350°.
• Line 2 rimmed baking sheets with parchment paper. Set aside.
• In a large bowl, combine flour, sugar, lemon zest, baking powder, and salt, whisking well. Using a pastry blender, cut butter into flour mixture until mixture resembles coarse crumbs. Add macadamia nuts, tossing to coat with flour. Set aside.
• In a measuring cup, combine 1 cup plus 2 tablespoons cream and lemon extract, whisking to blend. Add cream mixture to flour mixture, stirring until a dough forms. (If mixture seems dry, add more cream, 1 tablespoon at a time, until uniformly moist.)
• Turn dough out onto a lightly floured surface. Knead lightly 3 to 4 times. Using a rolling pin, roll dough to a ½-inch thickness. Using a 2-inch square cutter, cut squares from dough, rerolling scraps as necessary. Place scones 2 inches apart on prepared baking sheets.
• Brush with remaining 2 tablespoons cream.
• Bake until edges of scones are golden brown and a wooden pick inserted in the centers comes out clean, approximately 20 minutes.

Rosemary-Cheddar Scones

Yield: 13 to 15 scones
Preparation: 25 minutes
Bake: 13 minutes

2 cups bread flour
2 teaspoons baking powder
½ teaspoon salt
4 tablespoons cold salted butter, cut into pieces
1½ cups coarsely shredded sharp white Cheddar
  cheese
1 tablespoon minced fresh rosemary
1¼ cups plus 2 tablespoons cold heavy whipping
  cream, divided

• Preheat oven to 400°.
• Line 2 rimmed baking sheets with parchment paper. Set aside.
• In a large bowl, combine flour, baking powder, and salt, whisking well. Using a pastry blender, cut butter into flour mixture until mixture resembles coarse crumbs. Add cheese and rosemary, tossing to coat cheese with flour. Add 1¼ cups cream to flour mixture, stirring until a dough forms. (If mixture seems dry, add more cream, 1 tablespoon at a time, until uniformly moist.)
• Turn dough out onto a lightly floured surface. Knead lightly 3 to 4 times. Using a rolling pin, roll dough out to a ½-inch thickness. Using a 2¼-inch square cutter, cut squares from dough, rerolling scraps as necessary. Place scones 2 inches apart on prepared baking sheets.
• Brush tops of scones with remaining 2 tablespoons cream.
• Bake until edges of scones are golden brown and a wooden pick inserted in the centers comes out clean, approximately 14 minutes.
• Serve warm.

Banana-Pecan Scones

Yield: 16 scones
Preparation: 25 minutes
Bake: 13 minutes

2¼ cups all-purpose flour
½ cup sugar
2¼ teaspoons baking powder
½ teaspoon salt
4 tablespoons cold salted butter, cut into pieces
½ cup chopped toasted pecans
½ cup puréed banana (approximately 2 bananas)
¾ cup cold heavy whipping cream
¼ teaspoon banana extract
Garnish: 2 tablespoons turbinado sugar

• Preheat oven to 400°.
• Place 2 (8-well) wedge-shaped cast-iron scone pans*
in oven while it is heating.
• In a large bowl, combine flour, sugar, baking powder,
and salt, whisking well. Using a pastry blender, cut
butter into flour mixture until mixture resembles coarse
crumbs. Add pecans and puréed banana, stirring to
blend. Set aside.
• In a measuring cup, combine cream and banana
extract, stirring to blend. Add cream mixture all at once
to flour mixture, stirring until a dough forms. (If mixture
seems dry, add more cream, 1 tablespoon at a time,
until uniformly moist.)
• Remove preheated pans from oven. Spray pans
lightly with nonstick cooking spray.
• Using a levered 3-tablespoon scoop, divide dough
among wells of prepared pans. Using damp fingers,
carefully press dough into wells of pans, creating a
level surface. Sprinkle scones with turbinado sugar.
• Bake until scones are light golden brown and a
wooden pick inserted in the centers comes out clean,
13 to 15 minutes. Remove scones from pans.
• Serve immediately, or let cool on a wire rack.

*We used a Lodge 9-inch wedge pan, which is
available at lodgemfg.com.*

Honey-Ginger Scones

Yield: 16 to 18 scones
Preparation: 25 minutes
Bake: 12 minutes

1½ cups all-purpose flour
2 tablespoons sugar
2 teaspoons baking powder
¼ teaspoon salt
1 teaspoon ground ginger
1 teaspoon fresh lemon zest
4 tablespoons cold salted butter, cut into pieces
½ cup plus 3 tablespoons cold heavy whipping cream
2 tablespoons honey
1 recipe Honey Glaze (recipe follows)
Garnish: chopped crystallized ginger

• Preheat oven to 350°.
• Line 2 rimmed baking sheets with parchment paper.
Set aside.
• In a medium bowl, combine flour, sugar, baking powder, salt, ginger, and lemon zest, whisking well. Using
a pastry blender, cut butter into flour mixture until
mixture resembles coarse crumbs. Set aside.
• In a measuring cup, combine cream and honey. Add
to flour mixture, stirring until a dough forms. (If mixture
seems dry, add more cream, 1 tablespoon at a time,
until uniformly moist.)
• Using a levered 1½-tablespoon scoop, drop scones
2 inches apart onto prepared baking sheets.
• Bake until edges of scones are golden and a wooden
pick inserted in the centers comes out clean, 12 to 13
minutes. Transfer scones to a wire cooling rack, and
let cool completely.
• Spoon Honey Glaze over scones.
• Garnish with crystallized ginger while glaze is still
wet, if desired.

Honey Glaze

Yield: 1 cup
Preparation: 5 minutes

1½ cups confectioners' sugar
¼ cup whole milk
1 tablespoon honey

• In a small bowl, combine confectioners' sugar, milk,
and honey, whisking until smooth and creamy.
• Use immediately.

Savories

KITCHEN *Tip*

To make basil chiffonade, stack several basil leaves together, and roll into a cylinder. Starting from short end, cut into ⅛-inch slices.

Tuna-Avocado Tea Sandwiches

Yield: 4 tea sandwiches
Preparation: 25 minutes
Cook: 4 minutes

1 (6-ounce) fresh tuna fillet
3 teaspoons olive oil, divided
⅛ teaspoon garlic salt
⅛ teaspoon ground black pepper
⅛ teaspoon ground paprika
8 slices sourdough sandwich bread, such as
    Pepperidge Farm Farmhouse Sourdough
1 recipe Smoked Paprika Aïoli (recipe follows)
4 leaves butter lettuce
8 thin slices avocado, tossed in 1 tablespoon fresh
    lemon juice
½ cup alfalfa sprouts

• Drizzle both sides of tuna fillet with 2 teaspoons olive oil. Sprinkle both sides evenly with garlic salt, pepper, and paprika, rubbing spices into tuna.
• In a small nonstick skillet, heat remaining 1 teaspoon olive oil over medium-high heat. When oil shimmers, add tuna, and cook until charred, approximately 2 minutes per side.* Remove tuna from pan, and wrap in aluminum foil. Let rest until ready to slice.[†]
• Using a 2½-inch square cutter, cut 8 squares from bread slices. Spread Smoked Paprika Aïoli on a side of each bread square. Set aside.
• Using a sharp knife, slice tuna into ¼-inch-thick pieces. Set aside.
• Lay a leaf of butter lettuce on aïoli side of 4 bread squares. Arrange 3 tuna slices and 2 avocado slices in a shingled layer, alternating tuna and avocado atop lettuce. Top each evenly with sprouts, and cover with another bread square, aïoli side down. Secure with a decorative pick, if desired.
• Serve immediately.

Tuna should be cooked with a rare interior. If more doneness is desired, increase cooking time on each side.

[†]*Tuna may be served warm or cold. To chill, wrap securely in foil, and refrigerate earlier in the day. To slice tuna, use a sharp slicing knife, and cut across the grain into ¼-inch slices.*

Smoked Paprika Aïoli

Yield: ½ cup
Preparation: 5 minutes

½ cup mayonnaise
1 tablespoon plus 1 teaspoon creamy French dressing
2 teaspoons fresh lemon juice
¼ teaspoon smoked paprika

• In a small bowl, combine mayonnaise, French dressing, lemon juice, and paprika, whisking until smooth and creamy. Cover, and refrigerate until needed. (Aïoli may be made a day in advance.)

Apple-Basil Panini

Yield: 4 tea sandwiches
Preparation: 30 minutes
Cook: 4 minutes

2 red apples, such as Pink Lady
2 teaspoons fresh lemon juice
2 teaspoons creamy prepared horseradish
4 large, thin slices white sandwich bread
2 tablespoons fresh basil chiffonade (see Kitchen
    Tip on facing page)
4 ultrathin slices provolone cheese
4 teaspoons salted butter, softened
Garnish: apple slices, fresh basil

• Using a sharp knife, cut 4 wedges from each apple, discarding core. Cut ⅛-inch slices from each apple wedge. Reserve 12 slices for garnish, and toss them in lemon juice. Set aside.
• Spread horseradish onto 2 bread slices. Arrange apple slices on top of each bread slice in a shingled fashion. Sprinkle with basil chiffonade. Top each with 2 cheese slices and a bread slice. Lightly spread butter onto tops and bottoms of sandwiches.
• In a nonstick skillet or griddle, cook over medium-high heat until sandwiches are light golden brown on both sides and cheese melts. Transfer sandwiches to a cutting board.
• Using a 3-inch round cutter, cut 2 rounds from each sandwich, discarding crusts.
• Garnish with reserved apple slices and fresh basil, if desired.
• Serve immediately.

"The mere chink of cups
and saucers tunes the
mind to happy repose."

—George Gissing

Cucumber-Radish Tea Sandwiches with Shallot-Chive Aïoli

Yield: 8 tea sandwiches
Preparation: 25 minutes

⅓ cup mayonnaise
1 teaspoon finely chopped fresh chives
1 teaspoon fresh lemon juice
½ teaspoon minced shallot
⅛ teaspoon salt
⅛ teaspoon ground black pepper
4 slices white sandwich bread, such as
    Pepperidge Farm White
1 English cucumber
1 cup whole radishes
Garnish: 8 chive knots

• In a small bowl, combine mayonnaise, chives, lemon juice, shallot, salt, and pepper, stirring to blend. Set aside.
• Using a 1½-inch round cutter, cut 16 rounds from bread. Set aside.
• Using a sharp knife or mandoline*, cut 24 (⅛-inch) slices cucumber. Cut 16 (⅛-inch) slices radish. Set vegetable slices aside.
• Spread ¼ teaspoon aïoli onto a side of each bread round. On each of 8 bread rounds, stack slices of cucumber and radish in this manner: cucumber, radish, cucumber, radish, cucumber. Top each with another bread round, aïoli side down.
• Garnish with a chive knot, if desired.
• Serve immediately.

MAKE-AHEAD TIP: *Sandwiches can be made earlier in the day, covered with damp paper towels, and stored in an airtight container in the refrigerator until needed.*

KITCHEN TIP: *To make chive knots, blanch strands of fresh chives in boiling water for 30 seconds. Lay chives on paper towels. Tie a simple knot in each chive, and trim ends of chives to equal lengths.*

*An excellent mandoline to use is the Kyocera Adjustable Ceramic Slicer, available at surlatable.com.

White Pimento Cheese Finger Sandwiches

Yield: 15 finger sandwiches
Preparation: 25 minutes

8 ounces sharp white Cheddar cheese, finely shredded
3 tablespoons mayonnaise
3 tablespoons chopped pimientos
2 tablespoons sweet pickle relish
¼ teaspoon ground black pepper
15 slices very thin wheat sandwich bread, such as
    Pepperidge Farm Very Thin Wheat

• In a medium bowl, combine cheese, mayonnaise, pimientos, pickle relish, and pepper, stirring to blend.
• Spread 2 tablespoons pimento cheese on a bread slice. Top with another bread slice, and spread another 2 tablespoons pimento cheese on top. Top with a third bread slice. Repeat with remaining pimento cheese and bread.
• Using a serrated knife, trim and discard crusts from all sides of sandwiches. Cut three finger sandwiches from each whole sandwich.

MAKE-AHEAD TIP: *Sandwiches can be made earlier in the day, covered with damp paper towels, and stored in an airtight container in the refrigerator until needed.*

HELPFUL
How-tos

For step-by-step
assembly photos,
turn to page 130.

> "It's a very good English custom
> Though the weather be cold or hot.
> When you need a little pick-up,
> you'll find a little tea cup
> Will always hit the spot."
>
> John William "Long John" Baldry,
> "Everything Stops for Tea"

Salmon Rose Puffs

Yield: 12 tea sandwiches
Preparation: 30 minutes
Bake: 8 minutes
Cool: 15 minutes

½ (17.3-ounce) package frozen puff pastry (1 sheet),
   thawed
¼ cup mayonnaise
¼ teaspoon wasabi paste, such as S&B
1 (4-ounce) package thin-sliced smoked salmon
12 slices pickled ginger
⅓ cup watercress sprigs

• Preheat oven to 400°.
• Line a rimmed baking sheet with parchment paper.
• Using a 1½-inch square cutter, cut 12 squares from puff pastry. Place on prepared baking sheet.
• Bake until puffed and light golden brown, 8 to 10 minutes. Let cool completely.
• Cut a horizontal slit in each puff pastry square, being careful not to cut all the way through. Set aside.
• In a small bowl, combine mayonnaise and wasabi, stirring until blended. Place 1 teaspoon mayonnaise-wasabi mixture on bottom half of each pastry square.
• Cut 12 (3-x-1-inch) strips from salmon, and roll each into a rose shape, flaring out top edges. Roll each slice of pickled ginger into a cylinder, and insert into center of a salmon rose. Place a salmon rose atop mayonnaise mixture on each pastry square, and cover with top half of pastry. Arrange 2 watercress sprigs on either side of each salmon rose.
• Serve immediately.

MAKE-AHEAD TIP: *Pastry squares can be baked earlier in the day and stored in an airtight container until needed. Make salmon roses no more than an hour before anticipated serving time, and store in an airtight container in the refrigerator until needed.*

Watercress–Cottage Cheese Tea Sandwiches

Yield: 24 tea sandwiches
Preparation: 25 minutes

1 cup cottage cheese
⅓ cup sour cream
1 tablespoon mayonnaise
¼ teaspoon salt
¼ teaspoon ground black pepper
1 cup chopped watercress leaves
¼ cup golden raisins
2 tablespoons finely chopped celery
24 slices firm white sandwich bread, such as
   Pepperidge Farm
Garnish: watercress

• In a medium bowl, combine cottage cheese, sour cream, mayonnaise, salt, and pepper, stirring until blended. Add watercress, raisins, and celery, stirring until incorporated.
• Using a 1¾-inch round cutter, cut 48 rounds from bread. Spread approximately 1 tablespoon filling onto each of 24 bread rounds; top each with another bread round.
• Garnish each tea sandwich with watercress, if desired.
• Serve immediately.

MAKE AHEAD TIP: *Sandwiches can be made earlier in the day, covered with damp paper towels, placed in an airtight container, and refrigerated until needed. Garnish just before serving.*

Lemon-Caper Aïoli

Yield: ¼ cup
Preparation: 5 minutes

¼ cup mayonnaise
2 teaspoons fresh lemon juice
2 teaspoons capers
⅛ teaspoon ground black pepper

• In a small bowl, combine mayonnaise, lemon juice, capers, and pepper, stirring until blended. Cover, and refrigerate for up to a day.

Smoked Trout Tea Sandwiches

Yield: 12 tea sandwiches
Preparation: 25 minutes
Refrigerate: 4 hours

1 (8-ounce) package smoked trout fillets,
   such as Ducktrap River of Maine
½ cup mayonnaise
2 tablespoons creamy prepared horseradish
2 tablespoons capers
1 tablespoon fresh lemon juice
1 tablespoon minced fresh dill
¼ teaspoon ground black pepper
9 slices very thin wheat bread, such as
   Pepperidge Farm Very Thin Wheat
Garnish: fresh dill sprigs

• Remove and discard skin from trout. Flake trout with a fork into a medium bowl. Add mayonnaise, horse-radish, capers, lemon juice, minced dill, and pepper, stirring until well combined. Cover, and refrigerate until cold, approximately 4 hours.
• Spread 3 tablespoons trout salad on a bread slice. Top with another bread slice, and spread another 3 tablespoons trout salad on top. Top with a third bread slice. Repeat with remaining salad and bread.
• Using a sharp, serrated knife, trim and discard crusts from sandwiches. Cut each sandwich into quarters, forming 4 square sandwiches.
• Garnish each sandwich with a dill sprig, if desired.

MAKE-AHEAD TIP: *Trout salad can be made a day in advance and refrigerated overnight. Sandwiches can be assembled earlier in the day, covered with damp paper towels, and stored in an airtight container in the refrigerator. For best flavor, serve sandwiches the same day they are made.*

Smoked Salmon BLT Tea Sandwiches

Yield: 6 tea sandwiches
Preparation: 20 minutes

6 slices sourdough bread, such as Pepperidge Farm
   Farmhouse Sourdough
1 recipe Lemon-Caper Aïoli (recipe follows)
¼ cup frisée*
1 (4-ounce) package thinly sliced smoked salmon
12 slices campari tomatoes
6 slices pancetta, cooked

• Using a 2¼-inch round cutter, cut 12 rounds from bread slices. Toast bread rounds lightly.
• Spread Lemon-Caper Aïoli on a side of each toasted bread round. Divide frisée among 6 bread rounds, aïoli side up. Place a thin slice of salmon atop frisée. Top salmon with 2 tomato slices. Top with pancetta. Place a toasted bread round, aïoli side down, on top of pancetta. Secure each sandwich with a frilled pick.
• Serve immediately.

Frisée, a member of the chicory family, has delicately slender, curly leaves with a mildly bitter flavor. It can be found in the lettuce section of your grocery store's produce department.

Dilly Shrimp Salad Finger Sandwiches

Yield: 8 finger sandwiches
Preparation: 30 minutes
Refrigerate: 4 hours

2 quarts water
2¼ teaspoons salt, divided
½ teaspoon black peppercorns
1 bay leaf
1 pound medium shrimp, peeled and deveined,
½ cup mayonnaise
1 tablespoon fresh lime juice
1 tablespoon minced fresh dill
2 teaspoons minced fresh shallot
1 tablespoon minced celery
⅛ teaspoon ground black pepper
12 slices very thin white sandwich bread, such as
    Pepperidge Farm
Garnish: fresh dill sprigs

• In a medium saucepan, combine water, 2 teaspoons salt, peppercorns, and bay leaf. Bring to a boil over high heat. Remove from heat, and add shrimp. Cover, and poach for 5 minutes. (Shrimp should be pink/white and opaque.) Drain shrimp, and place in a bowl of ice water to stop cooking and to chill. Remove shrimp from ice water, and blot dry on paper towels.
• In the work bowl of a food processor, process shrimp until finely chopped.
• In a medium bowl, combine shrimp, mayonnaise, lime juice, dill, shallot, celery, remaining ¼ teaspoon salt, and pepper, stirring to combine. Place shrimp salad in a covered container, and refrigerate until cold, approximately 4 hours.
• For each sandwich, use 3 bread slices. Spread 3 tablespoons shrimp salad onto a bread slice. Top with another bread slice. Spread another 3 tablespoons shrimp salad onto that bread slice. Top with a third bread slice. Repeat with remaining salad and bread.
• Using a long serrated knife, trim and discard crusts from all sides of sandwiches. Cut each sandwich into 2 finger sandwiches.
• Garnish with dill sprigs, if desired.

MAKE-AHEAD TIP: *Sandwiches can be made earlier in the day, covered with damp paper towels, and stored in an airtight container in the refrigerator until ready to serve.*

Caprese Crostini

Yield: 24 canapés
Preparation: 20 minutes
Bake: 7 minutes

24 (¼-inch) slices French baguette
¼ cup olive oil
24 slices fresh mozzarella
⅓ cup fresh basil pesto, such as Buitoni
24 fresh basil leaves
24 slices cherry tomato
Garnish: fresh ground pepper

• Preheat oven to 350°.
• Line a rimmed baking sheet with parchment paper.
• Place baguette slices on prepared baking sheet. Lightly brush tops of bread with olive oil.
• Bake until light golden brown, approximately 7 minutes. Let cool.
• Using a 1½-inch flower-shaped cutter, cut 24 shapes from mozzarella, discarding scraps. Set aside.
• Spread approximately ½ teaspoon basil pesto onto each crostini. Lay a basil leaf on top of pesto, then a mozzarella flower, and then a tomato slice. Lightly brush each tomato with remaining olive oil, and sprinkle with fresh ground pepper.
• Serve immediately.

• Turn scallops over, and cook for exactly 1 minute on other side. During that minute, add butter and 1 tablespoon lime juice. As soon as butter melts, spoon juices over scallops as they cook. At the end of second minute, immediately transfer scallops to a plate lined with paper towels. (Exterior of scallop should look cara-melized, but interior should be tender and white.) Let scallops cool completely. Cover tightly, and refrigerate until cold, at least 4 hours.
• Using a sharp knife, cut scallops in half horizontally to make 12 scallops.
• In a small bowl, combine sweet chili sauce, soy sauce, and remaining 1 teaspoon lime juice, stirring to blend. Set aside.
• Place a chilled scallop on each rice cracker. Brush scallops with sweet chili glaze.
• Garnish with cilantro, if desired.
• Serve immediately.

MAKE-AHEAD TIP: *Scallops can be cooked earlier in the day and refrigerated until serving time. Sweet chili glaze can be made earlier in the day and refrigerated until serving time. Assemble canapés just before serving so rice crackers don't become soggy.*

Asian-Glazed Scallop Canapés

Yield: 12 canapés
Preparation: 20 minutes
Cook: 2 minutes
Refrigerate: 4 hours

2 tablespoons vegetable oil
6 large sea scallops
⅛ teaspoon fine sea salt
⅛ teaspoon ground black pepper
1 tablespoon butter
1 tablespoon plus 1 teaspoon fresh lime juice, divided
¼ cup Thai sweet chili sauce, such as Maggi Taste of Asia
1 teaspoon soy sauce
12 rice crackers with seaweed, such as Ka-Me
Garnish: fresh cilantro

• In a medium sauté pan, heat vegetable oil over high heat until it shimmers. Blot scallops dry on paper towels. Season with salt and pepper. Using tongs, place scallops in hot oil, and immediately reduce heat to medium. Let scallops cook, undisturbed, for exactly 1 minute.

Asparagus-Prosciutto Crostini

Yield: 12 canapés
Preparation: 25 minutes
Bake: 5 minutes

12 (¼-inch) slices French baguette
1 tablespoon olive oil
¼ cup cream cheese, softened
2 tablespoons finely chopped fresh asparagus
⅛ teaspoon ground black pepper
12 (6-x-1-inch) strips prosciutto
12 asparagus curls (see Kitchen Tip on facing page)

• Preheat oven to 350°.
• Line a rimmed baking sheet with parchment paper.
• Place baguette slices on prepared baking sheet. Lightly brush tops of bread with olive oil.
• Bake until light golden brown, approximately 5 min-utes. Let cool.
• In a small bowl, combine cream cheese, chopped asparagus, and pepper, stirring until blended. Spread 1 teaspoon cream-cheese mixture onto each cooled crostini. Ruffle a prosciutto strip onto each crostini. Top with a curl of asparagus.
• Serve immediately.

KITCHEN *Tip*

To make asparagus curls, shave a thin slice of asparagus from the stalk vertically, using a Y-shaped vegetable peeler. Wind asparagus pieces around a straw to make them curl.

Pineapple-Horseradish Glazed Pork Crostini with Slaw

Yield: 24 canapés
Preparation: 35 minutes
Bake: 20 minutes

1 (¾-pound) pork tenderloin
2 tablespoons plus 1 teaspoon olive oil, divided

¼ teaspoon garlic salt
¼ teaspoon ground black pepper
¼ teaspoon ground paprika
1 recipe Pineapple-Horseradish Glaze (recipe follows)
24 prepared French bread crostini
1 recipe Green and Purple Slaw (recipe follows)
Garnish: green onion slices

- Preheat oven to 350°.
- Line a rimmed baking sheet with aluminum foil.
- Place pork tenderloin on prepared baking sheet. Drizzle pork with 2 tablespoons olive oil. Sprinkle with garlic salt, pepper, and paprika, rubbing spices into meat.
- Bake for 20 minutes. (Pork will be very rare.) Let pork rest for 15 minutes before slicing. Using a sharp slicing knife, cut pork into 24 slices.
- Heat a large nonstick skillet over medium-high heat. Add remaining 1 teaspoon olive oil and pork slices. Sear for 1 minute per side to brown pork and finish cooking.
- Remove pan from heat. Add Pineapple-Horseradish Glaze to pan, tossing to coat pork slices.
- Place a pork slice on each crostini, and top evenly with Green and Purple Slaw.
- Garnish with green onion slices, if desired.

MAKE-AHEAD TIP: *Bake pork a day in advance, wrap in plastic wrap, and refrigerate until needed.*

Pineapple-Horseradish Glaze
Yield: 1 cup
Preparation: 5 minutes

½ cup pineapple preserves
½ cup apple jelly
1 teaspoon prepared horseradish
1 tablespoon fresh lime juice
½ teaspoon Dijon-style mustard

- In a small bowl, combine pineapple preserves, apple jelly, horseradish, lime juice, and mustard, stirring to blend.

Green and Purple Slaw
Yield: 1 cup
Preparation: 15 minutes
Refrigerate: 4 hours

2 tablespoons mayonnaise
2 teaspoons fresh lime juice
¼ teaspoon sugar
⅛ teaspoon salt
⅛ teaspoon ground black pepper
⅓ cup very finely chopped green cabbage
⅓ cup very finely chopped purple cabbage
¼ cup very finely chopped carrot
1 tablespoon finely chopped green onion

- In a medium bowl, combine mayonnaise, lime juice, sugar, salt, and pepper, whisking to blend. Add cabbages, carrot, and green onion, tossing to blend.

- Refrigerate slaw in a covered container until cold, approximately 4 hours

Ham, Olive, Pickle, and Nut Roulade
Yield: 8 rolled-sandwich bites
Preparation: 20 minutes
Refrigerate: 2 hours

1 (8-ounce) package cream cheese, softened
1 tablespoon heavy whipping cream
⅛ teaspoon ground black pepper
⅓ cup finely chopped pimiento-stuffed green olives
⅓ cup finely chopped dill pickles
⅓ cup finely chopped toasted pecans
1 (9-inch) flour tortilla
7 thin slices smoked deli ham

- In a small bowl, combine cream cheese, cream, and pepper. Beat at medium speed with an electric mixer until creamy and smooth. Add olives, pickles, and pecans, stirring to combine.
- Spread half of cream cheese mixture onto tortilla in an even layer. Lay ham slices over cream cheese layer, covering surface. Spread remaining cream cheese mixture over ham layer. Roll up filled tortilla tightly and evenly, and wrap securely in plastic wrap. Refrigerate for up to 2 hours before serving.
- To serve, unwrap roulade, and cut into ½-inch slices, using a serrated knife.

Chicken-Artichoke Salad in Melba Cups

Yield: 12 servings
Preparation: 20 minutes
Refrigerate: 4 hours

½ cup mayonnaise
1 teaspoon fresh lemon zest
1 tablespoon fresh lemon juice
1 teaspoon fresh lime zest
1 tablespoon fresh lime juice
½ teaspoon salt
⅛ teaspoon ground black pepper
3 cups chopped, roasted chicken, pulled from
   1 rotisserie chicken
½ cup chopped marinated artichokes
1 tablespoon chopped fresh dill
1 recipe Toasted Melba Cups (recipe follows)
Garnish: dill sprigs

• In a small bowl, combine mayonnaise, lemon zest, lemon juice, lime zest, lime juice, salt, and pepper, stirring until blended. Set aside.
• In a large bowl, combine chicken, artichokes, and dill, stirring until blended. Add mayonnaise mixture, stirring until chicken is uniformly moist. Cover, and refrigerate until cold, approximately 4 hours.
• Divide chicken salad evenly among Toasted Melba Cups.
• Garnish each serving with a dill sprig, if desired.

Toasted Melba Cups

Yield: 12 toast cups
Preparation: 10 minutes
Bake: 10 minutes
Cool: 20 minutes

12 very thin slices white sandwich bread, such as
   Pepperidge Farm
3 tablespoons butter, melted

• Preheat oven to 350°.
• Spray a standard 12-cup muffin pan with nonstick cooking spray. Set aside.
• Using a serrated knife, trim and discard crusts from bread slices. Using a rolling pin, flatten bread to make it flexible. Press a bread slice into each well of prepared muffin pan, forming a decorative cup. Brush bread lightly with melted butter.
• Bake until edges of bread are golden brown, approximately 10 minutes. Transfer toast cups to a wire rack, and let cool completely. Store in an airtight container at room temperature. (Toast cups are best made and eaten the same day.)

Pineapple-Pecan Tea Sandwiches

Yield: 24 tea sandwiches
Preparation: 30 minutes

48 slices very thin white sandwich bread, such as
   Pepperidge Farm Very Thin White
1 fresh pineapple, peeled and cored
1 (8-ounce) package cream cheese, softened
1 (6-ounce) can crushed pineapple, well drained
⅓ cup finely chopped toasted pecans

• Using a 2½-inch flower-shaped cutter, cut flower shapes from bread. Using a 1-inch round cutter, cut out the centers of half of bread slices, discarding centers. Keep bread flowers covered with damp paper towels to prevent drying out.
• Cut ¼-inch vertical slices from fresh pineapple. Using a 1-inch round cutter, cut 24 rounds from pineapple slices. Place on paper towels to absorb excess juice.
• In a medium bowl, combine cream cheese, crushed pineapple, and pecans, stirring until blended. Divide cream cheese mixture evenly among whole bread flowers, and spread. Top with bread flowers with centers cut out. Press pineapple rounds into centers of sandwiches.
• Store sandwiches, covered with damp paper towels, in an airtight container in the refrigerator until ready to serve, no more than 30 minutes.

MAKE-AHEAD
Tip

Chicken-Artichoke Salad
may be made a day in
advance and refriger-
ated until needed. Divide
among Toasted Melba
Cups just before serving.

Savory Crab and Corn Cheesecakes

Yield: 18 mini cheesecakes
Preparation: 30 minutes
Bake: 12 minutes
Cool: 1 hour

42 buttery round crackers, such as Ritz
½ cup plus 2 teaspoons butter, melted
2 (8-ounce) packages cream cheese, softened
2 large eggs
¼ cup all-purpose flour
1 tablespoon fresh lemon juice
½ teaspoon hot pepper sauce
½ teaspoon salt
⅛ teaspoon ground black pepper
1 (8-ounce) container cooked fresh jumbo lump
   crabmeat
½ cup fresh corn kernels
3 tablespoons finely chopped red bell pepper
1 tablespoon finely chopped fresh parsley
1 tablespoon finely chopped shallot
Garnish: fresh lemon zest, chopped parsley, chopped
   red bell pepper

- Preheat oven to 350°.
- Spray 18 wells of 2 (12-well) mini cheesecake pans with nonstick cooking spray. Set aside.
- In the work bowl of a food processor, pulse crackers until fine crumbs are formed.
- In a small bowl, combine cracker crumbs and melted butter, stirring until blended. Press 2 teaspoons crumb mixture into each prepared well of pans.
- Bake for 6 minutes.
- In a medium bowl, beat cream cheese at medium speed with an electric mixer until light and creamy, approximately 1 minute. Add eggs, beating just until incorporated. Add flour, lemon juice, hot pepper sauce, salt, and pepper, stirring until incorporated. Add crabmeat, corn, bell pepper, parsley, and shallot, stirring until incorporated.
- Using a levered 3-tablespoon scoop, divide crab mixture among prepared wells of pans.
- Bake until cheesecakes are set and slightly puffed, approximately 12 minutes. Let cool in pans for 1 hour before removing from pan.
- Garnish with lemon zest, parsley, and bell pepper, if desired.
- Serve warm.

MAKE-AHEAD TIP: *Cheesecakes may be made a day in advance, wrapped tightly while still in the pan, and refrigerated. Remove from pan, and place cheesecakes on a rimmed baking sheet in a 350° oven until warm, approximately 5 minutes.*

Ham Salad Tartlets

Yield: 20 tartlets
Preparation: 25 minutes
Bake: 7 minutes
Refrigerate: 4 hours

1 (14.1-ounce) package refrigerated pie dough (2 sheets)
2 cups chopped fully cooked ham steak
¼ cup mayonnaise
2 tablespoons spicy brown mustard
2 tablespoons finely chopped red bell pepper
1 tablespoon finely chopped sweet onion
½ teaspoon fresh thyme leaves
¼ teaspoon ground black pepper
¼ teaspoon ground paprika
⅛ teaspoon ground red pepper
Garnish: paprika and fresh thyme sprigs

- Preheat oven to 450°.
- Using a 2½-inch square cutter, cut 20 squares from pie dough. Press into 20 (2-inch) square tartlet pans with removable bottoms. Place tartlet pans on a rimmed baking sheet. Freeze for 15 minutes.
- Prick bottoms of tartlet shells with a fork to prevent puffing during baking.
- Bake for 5 minutes. Let cool completely on wire racks. Remove from tartlet pans.
- In the work bowl of a food processor, process ham until finely ground.
- In a medium bowl, combine ham, mayonnaise, mustard, bell pepper, onion, thyme, black pepper, paprika, and red pepper, stirring until blended. Cover, and refrigerate ham salad until cold, approximately 4 hours.
- Divide ham salad evenly among tartlet shells.
- Garnish with paprika and fresh thyme sprigs, if desired.

MAKE-AHEAD TIP: *Tartlet shells can be baked a day in advance and stored in an airtight container. Ham salad may be made earlier in the day and refrigerated until needed. Fill tartlet shells just before serving.*

Artichoke Tapenade Tartlets

Yield: 36 tartlets
Preparation: 25 minutes
Bake: 1 hour
Cool: 1 hour

1 (14.1-ounce) package refrigerated pie dough
  (2 sheets)
½ cup canned artichoke hearts, finely chopped
2 tablespoons finely chopped pimiento-stuffed
  green olives
2 tablespoons finely chopped fresh orange with peel
2 tablespoons olive oil
1 tablespoon finely chopped toasted almonds
1 tablespoon golden balsamic vinegar*, such as
  B.R. Cohn (available at *brcohn.com*)
½ teaspoon fresh thyme leaves
⅛ teaspoon ground black pepper
1/16 teaspoon ground red pepper
Garnish: finely chopped toasted almonds

• Preheat oven to 450°.
• On a lightly floured surface, unroll pie dough. Using
a 1¾-inch square cutter, cut 36 squares from dough.
Press into 36 (1½-x-1½-inch) tartlet pans, trimming
dough as necessary. Place tartlet pans on a rimmed
baking sheet. Refrigerate for 30 minutes.
• Prick bottoms of tartlet shells with a fork to prevent
puffing during baking.
• Bake until lightly browned, approximately 5 minutes.
Let tartlet shells cool completely; remove from pans.
• Reduce oven temperature to 300°.
• In a small bowl, combine artichokes, olives, orange,
olive oil, almonds, vinegar, thyme, black pepper, and
red pepper, stirring to blend. Place in a small ceramic
or glass baking dish, and cover tightly with foil.
• Bake for 1 hour. Let mixture cool completely, approx-
imately 30 minutes.
• Divide artichoke mixture evenly among tartlet shells.
• Garnish with finely chopped almonds, if desired.
• Serve immediately.

**Sherry vinegar may be substituted for golden
balsamic vinegar.*

MAKE-AHEAD TIP: *Tartlet shells can be made a day in
advance and stored in an airtight container. Artichoke
filling can be made a day in advance and refrigerated
in an airtight container. Let filling come to room temperature before using.*

Goat Cheese, Tomato, and Basil Croustades

Yield: 12 servings
Preparation: 15 minutes

4 ounces goat cheese, softened
4 teaspoons heavy whipping cream
1 tablespoon finely chopped smoked sun-dried
  tomatoes
½ teaspoon Italian seasoning
⅛ teaspoon ground black pepper
12 prepared croustades, such as Siljans
Garnish: 12 fresh basil leaves

• In a small bowl, combine goat cheese and cream.
Beat at medium speed with an electric mixer until
smooth and creamy. Add tomatoes, Italian seasoning,
and pepper beating until incorporated.
• Transfer mixture to a piping bag fitted with a small
open-star tip (Wilton #32). Evenly pipe mixture into
croustades, finishing with a decorative swirl.
• Garnish each croustade with a fresh basil leaf, if
desired.
• Serve immediately.

MAKE-AHEAD TIP: *Cheese mixture can be made a
day in advance and refrigerated overnight. Let come
to room temperature before piping. Fill croustades just
before serving.*

KITCHEN *Tip*

Use the pointed end
of a chopstick to press
exact indentations into
pie dough to create
beautiful tartlet shells.

Mini Quiches Lorraine

Yield: 12 mini quiches
Preparation: 30 minutes
Refrigerate: 30 minutes
Bake: 13 minutes
Cool: 40 minutes

1 (14.1-ounce) package refrigerated pie dough
  (2 sheets)
¾ cup finely grated Gruyère cheese
½ cup heavy whipping cream
1 large egg
¼ teaspoon salt
⅛ teaspoon ground black pepper
¹⁄₁₆ teaspoon ground nutmeg
¼ cup finely chopped cooked bacon

• Preheat oven to 450°.
• Line the bottoms of 12 (2¾-inch) round tartlet pans with parchment paper rounds. Set aside.
• Unroll both sheets of pie dough on a lightly floured surface. Using a 3½-inch round cutter, cut 12 rounds from pie dough. Press into prepared tartlet pans, and trim excess dough from edges. Place tartlet pans on a rimmed baking sheet. Refrigerate tartlet shells for 30 minutes. (This will help prevent shrinking during baking.)
• Prick bottoms of tartlet shells with a fork to prevent puffing while baking.
• Bake tartlet shells until light golden brown, approximately 7 minutes. Let cool completely.
• Reduce oven temperature to 350°.
• Divide cheese evenly among tartlet shells.
• In a measuring cup, combine cream, egg, salt, pepper, and nutmeg, whisking until well blended. Divide mixture evenly among tartlet shells. Sprinkle each quiche evenly with bacon.
• Bake until centers of quiches are set and slightly puffed, approximately 14 minutes. (Centers will fall as quiches cool.) Let cool in pans for 10 minutes. Carefully remove quiches from pans.
• Serve warm or at room temperature within 2 hours.

MAKE-AHEAD TIP: *Quiches may be made a day in advance, cooled completely, and then refrigerated overnight in an airtight container. Reheat in a 350° oven until warm, approximately 5 minutes.*

Zucchini, Feta, and Chive Quiche Bites

Yield: 24 servings
Preparation: 25 minutes
Bake: 12 minutes

1 teaspoon olive oil
2 cups (¼-inch) diced zucchini
½ cup crumbled feta cheese
⅛ cup chopped chives
3 large eggs
1 cup heavy whipping cream
½ teaspoon salt
¼ teaspoon dried thyme leaves
⅛ teaspoon ground black pepper
24 buttery round crackers, such as Ritz
Garnish: additional crumbled feta cheese

• Preheat oven to 350°.
• Spray a shallow 24-well mini muffin pan* with non-stick cooking spray. Set aside.
• In a medium nonstick sauté pan, heat olive oil over medium-high heat until it shimmers. Add zucchini, and sauté until lightly charred, 1 to 2 minutes. Reduce heat to low, cover, and let zucchini steam for 2 to 3 minutes. Divide zucchini evenly among wells of prepared pan.
• Add 1 teaspoon feta and ¼ teaspoon chives to each well. Set aside.
• In a 1-quart measuring cup, combine eggs, cream, salt, thyme, and pepper, whisking to blend. Divide mixture evenly among wells of prepared pan.
• Bake until quiches are set and slightly puffed, approximately 12 minutes. Let cool slightly in pan; remove from pan, and place quiches on crackers.
• Garnish with crumbled feta, if desired.
• Serve warm.

*We used a Chicago Metallic Nonstick 24-Cup Mini Muffin Pan, available at chicagometallicbakeware.com.

Caramelized Shallot and Blue Cheese Honeyed Swirls

Yield: 15 pastries
Preparation: 25 minutes
Bake: 13 minutes

1 tablespoon butter
1 teaspoon olive oil
1 cup (¼-inch) sliced shallots
1 large egg
1 tablespoon water
½ (17.3-ounce) package frozen puff pastry (1 sheet), thawed
⅓ cup blue cheese crumbles
¼ cup freshly grated Parmesan cheese
1 teaspoon fresh thyme leaves
⅛ teaspoon ground black pepper
⅓ cup honey
Garnish: fresh thyme sprigs

• Preheat oven to 400°.
• Line a rimmed baking sheet with parchment paper. Set aside.
• In a medium nonstick sauté pan, heat butter and olive oil over medium-high heat. Add shallots, and cook over low heat, stirring occasionally, until tender and light brown, approximately 10 minutes. Transfer to a bowl, and let cool. When cool, finely chop shallots. Set aside.
• In a small bowl, combine egg and water, whisking to blend.
• Place puff pastry on a lightly floured surface. Brush lightly with egg wash. Spread caramelized shallots over egg-wash layer. Sprinkle evenly with blue cheese, Parmesan cheese, thyme, and pepper. Roll filled puff pastry firmly and evenly, jelly-roll style, to form a cylinder. Using a serrated knife, cut into ½-inch slices. Place cut slices on prepared baking sheet, and brush tops with remaining egg wash.
• Bake until light golden brown, approximately 13 minutes. Remove pastries to a wire cooling rack, and let cool completely.
• Just before serving, brush pastries with honey.
• Garnish each with thyme sprigs, if desired.

MAKE-AHEAD TIP: *Puff pastry can be filled, rolled, and cut into ½-inch slices up to an hour in advance. Refrigerate until ready to bake.*

Apricot-Bacon Phyllo Cups

Yield: 18 tartlets
Preparation: 15 minutes

½ cup whole dried apricots
1 tablespoon chopped toasted pistachios
3 tablespoons blue cheese crumbles
2 tablespoons honey
2 tablespoons finely chopped cooked bacon
⅛ teaspoon freshly ground black pepper
18 mini phyllo cups, such as Athens
Garnish: chopped pistachios

• In the work bowl of a food processor, pulse apricots until very finely chopped.
• In a medium bowl, combine chopped apricots, pistachios, cheese, honey, bacon, and pepper, stirring to blend. Divide mixture evenly among phyllo cups.
• Garnish with chopped pistachios, if desired.
• Serve immediately.

KITCHEN *Tip*

A fine Microplane grater makes quick work of grating hard cheeses, such as Parmesan.

Frico Cups with Herbed Goat Cheese

Yield: 12 cups
Preparation: 25 minutes
Bake: 5 minutes

¾ cup freshly grated Parmesan cheese*
¼ cup goat cheese, at room temperature
2 teaspoons heavy whipping cream
1 teaspoon finely chopped fresh chives

1 teaspoon finely chopped fresh dill
1 teaspoon finely chopped fresh parsley
Garnish: fresh dill sprigs

• Preheat oven to 350°.
• Line a rimmed baking sheet with parchment paper or a silicone baking mat.
• Sprinkle Parmesan cheese in 6 (2½-inch) circles onto prepared baking sheet.

- Bake until cheese melts and is very light brown, approximately 5 minutes. Remove from oven. Quickly lift from baking sheet, and drape over backs of mini muffin pans to form cups. Let cool completely. Repeat with remaining cheese. (Cheese cups can be made earlier in the day and kept in an airtight container.)
- In a small bowl, combine goat cheese and cream. Beat at low speed with an electric mixer until smooth and creamy. Add chives, dill, and parsley, stirring until incorporated.
- Using a levered 1-teaspoon scoop, place balls of goat cheese mixture into frico cups.
- Garnish with dill, if desired.

For the success of this recipe, it is important to use freshly grated cheese and not pregrated cheese.

Tomato Rose with Shrimp Couscous Salad

Yield: 12 servings
Preparation: 35 minutes
Cook: 5 minutes
Refrigerate: 4 hours

3 cups water
2¼ teaspoons Old Bay Seasoning, divided
1 bay leaf
2 slices fresh lemon
1 cup medium shrimp, peeled and deveined
½ cup bottled clam juice
½ cup couscous
2 tablespoons finely chopped celery
2 tablespoons frozen baby green peas, defrosted
2 tablespoons golden balsamic vinegar, such as B.R. Cohn (available at *brcohn.com*)
1 tablespoon finely chopped green onion (green tops only)
1 tablespoon lemon olive oil[†], such as B.R. Cohn (available at *brcohn.com*)
¼ teaspoon salt
⅛ teaspoon ground black pepper
12 Campari tomatoes
Garnish: fresh basil leaves

- In a medium saucepan, combine water, 2 teaspoons Old Bay Seasoning, bay leaf, and lemon slices. Bring to a boil over high heat. Remove from heat, and add shrimp. Cover, and poach for 5 minutes. (Shrimp should be pink/white and opaque.) Drain shrimp, and place in a bowl of ice water to stop cooking. Remove shrimp from ice water, and blot dry on paper towels. Chop shrimp very finely. Set aside.

- In a small saucepan, bring clam juice to a boil. Add couscous, and remove pan from heat. Cover, and let stand for 4 minutes to cook couscous.
- Transfer couscous to a medium bowl, and fluff with a fork. Add chopped shrimp, celery, green peas, vinegar, green onion, olive oil, remaining ¼ teaspoon Old Bay Seasoning, salt, and pepper, tossing with a fork to combine. Refrigerate until cold, at least 4 hours.
- Using a small serrated knife, make cuts in tomatoes to resemble a rose, cutting off tops of tomatoes and coring inside. (See step-by-step How-to on page 130.) Blot dry on paper towels.
- Divide Shrimp Couscous Salad evenly among tomatoes.
- Garnish each tomato with a fresh basil leaf, if desired.

White balsamic vinegar can be substituted for golden balsamic vinegar.

[†]*Regular extra-virgin olive oil can be substituted for lemon olive oil.*

Sweets

"Another novelty is the tea-party, an extraordinary meal in that, being offered to persons that have already dined well, it supposes neither appetite nor thirst, and has no object but distraction, no basis but delicate enjoyment."

—Jean Anthelme Brillat-Savarin

Lemon French Macarons

Yield: 30 sandwich cookies
Preparation: 5 hours
Bake: 24 minutes per batch

3 large egg whites
1 cup toasted slivered almonds
2 cups confectioners' sugar*
2 tablespoons sugar
½ teaspoon lemon extract
Lemon yellow paste food coloring, such as Wilton
¾ cup prepared lemon curd

• Place egg whites in a medium bowl, and let sit at room temperature, uncovered, for exactly 3 hours. (Aging the egg whites in this manner is essential to creating perfect French macarons.)
• Line several baking sheets with parchment paper. Using a pencil, draw 1½-inch circles 2 inches apart on parchment paper. Turn parchment paper over. Set aside.
• In the work bowl of a food processor, combine almonds and 1 tablespoon confectioners' sugar, pulsing until very finely ground. (Don't overprocess or a nut butter will be created. The nut particles should stay separate and dry but not clump together.) Add remaining confectioners' sugar, and process just until combined. Set aside.
• Beat egg whites at medium-high speed with an electric mixer until frothy. Gradually add sugar, beating at high speed until stiff peaks form, 3 to 5 minutes. (Egg whites will be thick, creamy, and shiny.) Add lemon extract, beating well.

• Using a toothpick, add food coloring, a small amount at a time, beating until desired color is achieved.
• Add almond mixture to egg whites, folding gently by hand until well combined. Let batter sit for 15 minutes.
• Transfer batter to a pastry bag fitted with a medium round tip (Wilton #12). Pipe batter into drawn circles onto prepared baking sheets.
• Slam baking sheets vigorously on counter 5 to 7 times to release air bubbles.
• Let sit at room temperature for 45 to 60 minutes before baking to help develop the macaron's signature crisp exterior when baked. (Macarons should feel dry to the touch and should not stick to finger.)
• Preheat oven to 275°.
• Bake until firm to the touch, approximately 24 minutes.
• Let cool completely on pans, and then transfer to air-tight containers. Refrigerate until ready to fill and serve.
• Place lemon curd in a pastry bag fitted with a small round tip. Pipe curd onto flat side of a macaron, and top with another macaron, flat sides together, pushing down lightly and twisting so curd spreads to edges. Repeat with remaining macarons and lemon curd.
• Serve immediately, or refrigerate in an airtight container for up to 3 days. Let come to room temperature before serving.

To measure confectioners' sugar accurately, spoon lightly into measuring cup, and level off, using a straight edge. Do not pack or scoop sugar into cup as this will negatively affect final product.

Pumpkin-Chai Bars with Pecan Shortbread Crust

Yield: 35 bars
Preparation: 30 minutes
Bake: 45 minutes
Refrigerate: 4 hours

1 cup all-purpose flour
½ cup toasted pecan halves
½ teaspoon salt, divided
½ cup salted butter, softened
1 cup firmly packed light brown sugar, divided
1¼ teaspoons vanilla extract, divided
2 large eggs, lightly beaten
1 (15-ounce) can pumpkin
1¼ cups heavy whipping cream
¼ cup maple syrup
1 teaspoon ground cinnamon
½ teaspoon ground ginger
½ teaspoon ground cardamom
⅛ teaspoon ground nutmeg
1 recipe Vanilla Whipped Cream (recipe follows)
Garnish: ground nutmeg

• Preheat oven to 350°.
• Line a 13-x-9-inch baking pan with heavy-duty aluminum foil, letting foil hang over sides of pan to create handles. Line foil with parchment paper; spray lightly with nonstick cooking spray. Set aside.
• In the work bowl of a food processor, combine flour, pecans, and ¼ teaspoon salt; pulse until pecans are finely ground. Set aside.
• In a medium bowl, combine butter, ½ cup brown sugar, and ¾ teaspoon vanilla extract. Beat at medium speed with an electric mixer until creamy. Add flour mixture, beating until mixture resembles coarse crumbs. Press evenly into bottom of prepared pan, smoothing to create a level surface.
• Bake until golden brown, approximately 15 minutes. Let cool completely.
• In a medium bowl, combine eggs, pumpkin, cream, remaining ½ cup brown sugar, maple syrup, remaining ½ teaspoon vanilla extract, cinnamon, ginger, cardamom, remaining ¼ teaspoon salt, and nutmeg, stirring to blend. Pour over cooled crust, smoothing to create a level surface.
• Bake until set, approximately 30 minutes. Let cool completely. Refrigerate, covered, until cold, approximately 4 hours.
• Lift from pan, using foil handles, and place on a cutting surface. Cut into 35 bars.
• Place Vanilla Whipped Cream in a piping bag fitted with a small open-star tip (Wilton #32). Pipe in a decorative swirl onto each bar.

• Garnish with a sprinkling of ground nutmeg, if desired.
• Serve immediately.

MAKE-AHEAD TIP: *Pumpkin-Chai Bars can be made a day in advance and refrigerated in pan overnight. Cut, pipe Vanilla Whipped Cream onto bars, and garnish with nutmeg (if desired), just before serving.*

Vanilla Whipped Cream

Yield: 1½ cups
Preparation: 5 minutes

¾ cup cold heavy whipping cream
2 tablespoons confectioners' sugar
½ teaspoon vanilla extract

• In a medium bowl, combine cream, confectioners' sugar, and vanilla extract. Beat at high speed with an electric mixer until thick and creamy. Refrigerate until needed.

Lemon-Rosemary Linzer Cookies

Yield: 42 sandwich cookies
Preparation: 35 minutes
Refrigerate: 1 hour 15 minutes
Bake: 9 to 10 minutes

1 cup salted butter, softened
¾ cup sugar
2 teaspoons fresh lemon zest
½ teaspoon vanilla extract
¼ teaspoon lemon extract
2¼ cups all-purpose flour
2 teaspoons finely minced fresh rosemary
¼ teaspoon salt
1 tablespoon heavy whipping cream
1 cup prepared lemon curd

• Preheat oven to 350°.
• Line 2 rimmed baking sheets with parchment paper. Set aside.
• In a medium bowl, combine butter and sugar. Beat at medium-high speed with an electric mixer until light and creamy. Add lemon zest, vanilla extract, and lemon extract, beating until incorporated. Set aside.
• In a small bowl, combine flour, rosemary, and salt, whisking well. Add flour mixture to butter mixture, beating at low speed until incorporated. Add cream, beating until dough comes together.
• Divide dough in half. Turn each section out onto a sheet of plastic wrap, and wrap securely. Refrigerate for 1 hour.
• On a lightly floured surface, roll dough with a rolling pin to a ⅛-inch thickness. Using a 1¾-inch round cutter, cut 84 rounds from dough, rerolling scraps as necessary. Work quickly so that dough doesn't get too warm. Refrigerate dough, if necessary. Transfer cookies to prepared baking sheets.
• Using a diamond-shaped linzer cutter, cut holes in the centers of 42 cookies. Refrigerate cookies on pans for 15 minutes. (This will prevent cookies from spreading while baking.)
• Bake until edges of cookies are light golden brown, 9 to 10 minutes. Transfer cookies to a wire rack, and let cool completely.
• Spread 1 teaspoon lemon curd onto cookies with no cutouts. Top with cutout cookies.
• Refrigerate in an airtight container for no more than 4 hours before serving.

Coconut Macaroons with Pineapple Jam

Yield: 44 cookies
Preparation: 25 minutes
Bake: 17 minutes

1 (14-ounce) package sweetened, flaked coconut
⅔ cup sugar
6 tablespoons all-purpose flour
¼ teaspoon salt
4 large egg whites
1 cup pineapple jam

• Preheat oven to 325°.
• Line 2 baking sheets with parchment paper. Set aside.
• In the work bowl of a food processor, pulse coconut 4 to 5 times until finely chopped.
• In a medium bowl, combine chopped coconut, sugar, flour, and salt, whisking to blend. Add egg whites, stirring until incorporated.
• Using a levered 2-teaspoon scoop, drop cookie dough 2 inches apart onto prepared baking sheets. Using a finger or the back of a rounded measuring spoon, press an indentation into each cookie.
• Bake until cookies are set and edges are golden brown, approximately 17 minutes. Transfer cookies to a wire rack, and let cool completely. Store in an airtight container at room temperature until ready to fill with jam.
• Just before serving, place 1 teaspoon pineapple jam into the indentation on each cookie.

MAKE-AHEAD TIP: *Cookies can be baked a week in advance, and stored, unfilled, in an airtight container in the freezer. Fill with pineapple jam just before serving.*

Lemon–Poppy Seed Sandwich Cookies

Yield: 21 sandwich cookies
Preparation: 30 minutes
Bake: 10 minutes

1¼ cups all-purpose flour
½ teaspoon baking soda
¼ teaspoon salt
½ cup salted butter, softened
½ cup sugar
1 large egg
1 tablespoon fresh lemon zest
½ teaspoon vanilla extract
2 tablespoons poppy seeds
1 recipe Lemon Buttercream (recipe follows)
Garnish: fresh purslane

• Preheat oven to 350°.
• Line 2 rimmed baking sheets with parchment paper. Set aside.
• In a medium bowl, combine flour, baking soda, and salt, whisking well. Set aside.
• In a large bowl, combine butter and sugar. Beat at high speed with an electric mixer until light and creamy, approximately 3 minutes. Add egg, lemon zest, and vanilla extract, beating until incorporated. Add flour mixture, beating until incorporated and scraping down sides of bowl as necessary. Reduce mixer to low speed, and add poppy seeds, beating just until incorporated.
• Using a levered 1-teaspoon scoop, drop dough 2 inches apart onto prepared baking sheets.
• Bake until edges are light golden brown, approximately 10 minutes. Transfer cookies to a wire rack, and let cool completely.
• Place Lemon Buttercream in a piping bag fitted with a medium open tip (Wilton #12). Pipe a 1-inch button of buttercream onto flat side of a cookie. Top with another cookie, flat side down. Twist top cookie slightly to spread buttercream to edges of cookie. Repeat with remaining cookies and buttercream. Refrigerate in an airtight container for up to 3 days.
• Garnish with fresh purslane before serving, if desired.

MAKE-AHEAD TIP: *Cookies can be made a week in advance and frozen, unfilled, in an airtight container. Fill with buttercream before serving.*

KITCHEN TIP: *If baking more than one pan of cookies at the same time, rotate baking sheets from top rack to bottom rack halfway through baking time.*

Lemon Buttercream Filling

Yield: 1 cup
Preparation: 5 minutes

1½ cups confectioners' sugar
½ cup salted butter, softened
1 teaspoon lemon extract

• In a large bowl, combine confectioners' sugar, butter, and lemon extract. Beat with an electric mixer, starting at low speed and gradually increasing to high speed, until buttercream is light and fluffy.
• Use immediately, or refrigerate in an airtight container until needed. Let buttercream come to room temperature before using.

GARNISHING WITH FLOWERS

• Use only edible flowers as a garnish. If your guests find a flower on their plates, they will assume it can be eaten. Commonly grown edible flowers include daylilies, impatiens, purslane, roses, and violets. Beware of flowers that have similar names but may be from a different genus. For example, pansies, violets, and violas, which all belong to the genus *Viola*, are edible; African violets from the genus *Saintpaulia* are not.

• When purchasing flowers for culinary use, buy them from a supplier who grows flowers specifically for consumption. Such flowers are often sold at gourmet markets. Do not use flowers that have been treated with pesticides, and do not purchase flowers from a florist.

• One way to guarantee edible flowers are completely pesticide-free is to grow them yourself. Pick homegrown flowers in the morning or late afternoon when the water content is high. Select flowers that have just opened and are free of spots. Store flowers in a glass of water in the refrigerator until you are ready to use them, and use them within a few hours.

- Preheat oven to 350°.
- Line a 13-x-9-inch baking pan with heavy-duty aluminum foil, letting foil hang over sides of pan to create handles. Spray with nonstick cooking spray. Set aside.
- In a medium bowl, combine flour, sugar, cocoa, brown sugar, and baking powder, whisking well. Set aside.
- In a large bowl, combine melted butter, eggs, and vanilla extract, stirring with a spoon to blend. Add flour mixture, stirring to incorporate. Pour batter into prepared pan, smoothing and leveling surface with a spatula.
- Bake until a wooden pick inserted in the center of brownie comes out with just a few crumbs clinging to it, approximately 25 minutes. Let brownie cool completely in pan.
- Using an offset spatula, spread warm Semisweet Ganache evenly and smoothly over surface of brownie. Sprinkle evenly with pistachios, if desired.
- Refrigerate brownie until ganache is cold and solid, approximately 4 hours.
- Lift brownie from pan, using foil handles, and place on a cutting surface. Using a long knife, cut brownie into 40 pieces.
- Refrigerate in an airtight container for up to 2 days. Let come to room temperature before serving.

KITCHEN TIP: *When cutting brownies, press downward with knife to create sharp, clean edges.*

Semisweet Brownies with Pistachios

Yield: 40 bars
Preparation: 25 minutes
Bake: 25 minutes
Refrigerate: 4 hours

2 cups all-purpose flour
1½ cups sugar
½ cup natural unsweetened cocoa powder
¼ cup firmly packed light brown sugar
2 teaspoons baking powder
¾ cup salted butter, melted
3 large eggs
2 teaspoons vanilla extract
1 recipe Semisweet Ganache (recipe follows)
Garnish: finely chopped pistachios

Semisweet Ganache

Yield: ½ cup
Preparation: 10 minutes

½ cup plus 2 tablespoons heavy whipping cream
1 (4-ounce) bar semisweet chocolate, such as
   Ghirardelli, finely chopped

- Place chocolate in a heatproof bowl. Set aside.
- In a small saucepan, scald cream over medium-high heat. Pour over chopped chocolate, and let sit for 1 minute to allow chocolate to melt. Whisk until smooth and creamy.
- Use immediately.

"A Proper Tea is much nicer than a Very Nearly Tea, which is one you forget about afterwards."

A.A. Milne

Peanut Butter Blondies

Yield: 24 bars
Preparation: 25 minutes
Bake: 20 minutes

½ cup salted butter, softened
1 cup firmly packed light brown sugar
⅓ cup sugar
2 large eggs
2 teaspoons vanilla extract
2 cups all-purpose flour
2 teaspoons baking powder
½ teaspoon salt
1 cup chopped peanut-butter-cup candy, such as
 Reese's Miniatures
½ cup plus 1 tablespoon finely chopped dry-roasted,
 unsalted peanuts, divided
1 recipe Peanut Butter Whipped Cream (recipe
 follows)

• Preheat oven to 350°.
• Line a 13-x-9-inch baking pan with heavy-duty aluminum foil, letting foil hang over sides of pan to create handles. Spray with nonstick cooking spray. Set aside.
• In a large bowl, combine butter, light brown sugar, and sugar. Beat at medium speed with an electric mixer until fluffy. Add eggs, one at a time, beating until incorporated. Add vanilla extract, beating until combined. Set aside.
• In a medium bowl, combine flour, baking powder, and salt, whisking to blend. Add flour mixture to butter mixture. Beat with an electric mixer until incorporated, beginning at low speed and gradually increasing to medium speed. Add candy and ⅓ cup peanuts, stirring to blend. Spread batter into prepared pan, and smooth surface with a spatula. Reserving 1 tablespoon peanuts for garnish, sprinkle remaining peanuts evenly over batter.
• Bake until edges of blondie are golden brown and a toothpick inserted in the center comes out clean, approximately 20 minutes. Let cool completely in pan.
• Lift blondie from pan, using foil handles, and place on a cutting surface. Using a long knife, cut blondie into 24 squares.
• Place Peanut Butter Whipped Cream in a piping bag fitted with a small open-star tip (Wilton #32), and pipe onto blondie squares. (Blondies are best when served the day they are made.)
• Garnish with reserved 1 tablespoon peanuts, if desired.

Peanut Butter Whipped Cream

Yield: 1 cup
Preparation: 5 minutes

½ cup cold heavy whipping cream
1 tablespoon confectioners' sugar
¼ teaspoon vanilla extract
1 tablespoon creamy peanut butter

• In a small bowl, combine cream, confectioners' sugar, and vanilla extract. Beat at high speed with an electric mixer until stiff peaks form. Add peanut butter, beating until incorporated.
• Use immediately.

Cranberry Crumb Bars

Yield: 10 bars
Preparation: 35 minutes
Cook: 10 minutes
Bake: 40 minutes

1½ cups all-purpose flour
¾ cup quick oats
¾ cup firmly packed light brown sugar
¼ teaspoon ground mace
¾ cup cold salted butter
4 cups fresh or frozen cranberries
1 cup water
½ cup sugar
1 tablespoon cornstarch
½ teaspoon ground cinnamon
¼ cup maple syrup
1 teaspoon vanilla extract

• Preheat oven to 350°.
• Line an 8-inch square pan with heavy-duty aluminum foil, letting foil hang over sides of pan to create handles. Line foil with parchment paper; spray lightly with nonstick cooking spray. Set aside.
• In a large bowl, combine flour, oats, brown sugar, and mace, stirring well. Using a pastry blender, cut butter into flour mixture until mixture resembles coarse crumbs. Work mixture with fingers until mixture is uniformly moist.
• Reserve ¾ cup crumb mixture for topping. Press remaining crumb mixture into bottom of prepared baking pan, smoothing to create a level surface. Set aside.
• In a medium saucepan, combine cranberries, water, sugar, cornstarch, and cinnamon. Bring to a boil over high heat, stirring frequently. When mixture boils, reduce heat to low, but let mixture simmer until cranberries burst and mixture thickens, approximately 10 minutes. Remove from heat. Add maple syrup and vanilla extract, stirring until incorporated. Let mixture cool.
• Pour cranberry mixture over crumb crust, smoothing to create a level surface. Sprinkle with reserved crumbs.
• Bake until bars are set and crumb topping is golden brown, approximately 40 minutes. Let cool completely.
• Lift from pan using foil handles, and place on a cutting surface. Using a long knife, cut into bars.
• Store in an airtight container at room temperature.

MAKE-AHEAD TIP: *Cranberry bars can be made a week in advance and frozen in an airtight container. Cut into serving pieces while frozen. Let thaw before serving.*

KITCHEN TIP: *To cool cranberry mixture quickly, place bowl in a larger bowl filled with ice and water, and stir frequently.*

Cranberry–White Chocolate Cookies

Yield: 60 cookies
Preparation: 15 minutes
Bake: 7 minutes

1 cup plus 2 tablespoons all-purpose flour
½ teaspoon baking soda
½ teaspoon salt
½ cup salted butter, softened
⅓ cup sugar
½ cup firmly packed brown sugar
1 large egg
½ teaspoon vanilla extract
½ cup dried cranberries
⅓ cup finely chopped white chocolate
¼ cup finely chopped toasted pecans

• Preheat oven to 375°.
• Line 2 rimmed baking sheets with parchment paper. Set aside.
• In a medium bowl, combine flour, baking soda, and salt, whisking well. Set aside.
• In a medium bowl, combine butter, sugar, and brown sugar. Beat at high speed with an electric mixer until fluffy. Add egg and vanilla extract, beating at low speed until incorporated. Add flour mixture, beating at low to medium speed until incorporated. Add cranberries, white chocolate, and pecans, stirring to combine.
• Using a levered 1-teaspoon scoop, drop dough 2 inches apart onto prepared baking sheets.
• Bake until edges of cookies are golden brown, approximately 7 minutes. Transfer cookies to wire racks, and let cool completely.
• Store in airtight containers at room temperature for up to 3 days.

MAKE-AHEAD TIP: *Cookies can be made a week in advance and frozen in airtight containers until needed.*

KITCHEN *Tip*

For pretty bars,
freeze whole,
and cut into bars
while frozen.

Butterscotch–Vanilla Bean Meringue Tartlets

Yield: 12 tartlets
Preparation: 30 minutes
Bake: 8 minutes
Refrigerate: 4 hours

12 (3.15-inch) sweet tart shells, such as Clearbrook
    Farms
¼ cup salted butter
1 cup firmly packed light brown sugar
1¼ cups whole milk, divided
½ cup heavy whipping cream
1 large egg
1 large egg yolk
3 tablespoons cornstarch
¼ teaspoon salt
1 vanilla bean, split, seeds scraped and reserved
1 recipe Meringue (recipe follows)

• Preheat oven to 350°.
• Line a rimmed baking sheet with parchment paper. Arrange tart shells on pan. Set aside.
• In a medium saucepan, melt butter over low heat. Add brown sugar, stirring to combine. Cook and stir until sugar is melted and mixture is thick and creamy, approximately 3 minutes. Add ¾ cup milk and cream. Increase heat to medium, and bring to a boil, whisking constantly. Remove from heat
• In a medium bowl, combine egg, egg yolk, and remaining ½ cup milk, whisking well. Add cornstarch and salt, whisking to combine. Gradually add hot milk

mixture in a slow stream to egg mixture, whisking constantly. Add reserved vanilla-bean seeds, whisking well. Return mixture to saucepan, and cook over medium-low heat, whisking constantly until pudding thickens, 3 to 4 minutes. Divide custard evenly among tart shells.
• Place Meringue in a piping bag fitted with a large open-star tip (Wilton #1M). Pipe onto tartlets in a decorative swirl pattern resembling a rose.
• Bake tartlets until Meringue is brown, 8 to 10 minutes. Transfer tartlets to a wire cooling rack, and let cool completely. Refrigerate, covered, until cold, approximately 4 hours.
• Serve cold.

MAKE-AHEAD TIP: *Butterscotch–Vanilla Bean Meringue Tartlets can be made a day in advance and refrigerated until serving time.*

Meringue

Yield: 3 cups
Preparation: 5 minutes
Bake: 10 minutes

3 large egg whites
⅓ cup sugar
½ teaspoon cream of tartar

• In a large bowl, beat egg whites at high speed with an electric mixer until foamy. Add sugar and cream of tartar, beating until thick and fluffy, 2 to 3 minutes.
• Use immediately.

pressing down centers. Let cool in pan for 5 minutes. Carefully remove from pan, and let cool completely on a wire rack. Store tartlet shells in an airtight container for up to a day.
• In a small bowl, combine lemon curd and mascarpone cheese, stirring until smooth and creamy. Place in a covered container, and refrigerate until cold, approximately 4 hours.
• Transfer lemon curd mixture to a piping bag fitted with an open-star tip (Wilton #32). Pipe evenly into tartlet shells in a decorative swirl.
• Garnish with fresh mint, if desired.
• Serve immediately.

MAKE-AHEAD TIP: *Tartlet shells can be made a week in advance and frozen in an airtight container. Let thaw before filling.*

Chocolate-Cinnamon-Pecan Tartlets
Yield: 11 tartlets
Preparation: 25 minutes
Bake: 13 minutes
Refrigerate: 30 minutes
Cool: 1 hour

1 (14.1-ounce) package refrigerated pie dough
  (2 sheets)
1 large egg
½ cup firmly packed light brown sugar
3 tablespoons light corn syrup
1 tablespoon melted butter
1 teaspoon vanilla extract
½ teaspoon ground cinnamon
⅛ teaspoon salt
½ cup finely chopped toasted pecans
⅓ cup finely chopped semisweet chocolate, such as
  Ghirardelli
1 recipe Sweetened Whipped Cream (recipe follows)
Garnish: chocolate shavings

• Preheat oven to 450°.
• Line bottoms of 11 (2¾-inch) fluted tartlet pans with parchment paper rounds. Set aside.
• On a lightly floured surface, unroll pie dough. Using a 3-inch round cutter, cut 11 rounds from pie dough. Press into bottom and up sides of prepared tartlet pans. Place pans on a rimmed baking sheet. Refrigerate for 30 minutes.
• Prick bottoms of tartlet shells with a fork to prevent puffing during baking.
• Bake until very lightly browned, approximately 7 minutes. Let cool completely on wire racks.
• In a medium bowl, combine egg, brown sugar, corn

Lemon-Mascarpone Tartlets
Yield: 24 tartlets
Preparation: 25 minutes
Bake: 10 minutes
Refrigerate: 4 hours

½ cup salted butter, softened
½ cup sugar
1 large egg
½ teaspoon vanilla extract
1½ cups all-purpose flour
½ teaspoon baking powder
¼ teaspoon salt
1 (10-ounce) jar lemon curd, such as Dickinson's
¾ cup mascarpone cheese
Garnish: fresh mint

• Preheat oven to 375°.
• Spray a 24-well mini muffin pan with nonstick cooking spray. Set aside.
• In a medium bowl, combine butter and sugar. Beat at medium speed with an electric mixer until creamy. Add egg and vanilla extract, beating to combine. Set aside.
• In a small bowl, combine flour, baking powder, and salt, whisking well. Gradually add flour mixture to butter mixture, beating until combined.
• Divide dough into 1-inch balls. Press into wells of prepared pan, forming tartlet shells.
• Bake until edges of tartlet shells are light golden brown, approximately 10 minutes. Using a rounded spoon, immediately shape warm shells again by

syrup, butter, vanilla extract, cinnamon, and salt, whisking well. Add pecans and chocolate, stirring to combine. Divide mixture evenly among prepared tartlet pans.
• Reduce oven temperature to 350°.
• Bake tartlets until set and slightly puffed, approximately 13 minutes. Let cool completely. Gently remove from tartlet pans.
• Place Sweetened Whipped Cream in a piping bag fitted with a small open-star tip (Wilton #32). Pipe a decorative swirl of whipped cream onto each tartlet.
• Garnish with chocolate shavings, if desired.
• Serve immediately.

Sweetened Whipped Cream
Yield: 1 cup
Preparation: 5 minutes

½ cup cold heavy whipping cream
1 tablespoon confectioners' sugar
¼ teaspoon vanilla extract

• In a small bowl, combine cream, confectioners' sugar, and vanilla extract. Beat at high speed with an electric mixer until thickened and creamy. Refrigerate until needed.

Chocolate-Coconut Shortbread Tartlets

Yield: 5 tartlets
Preparation: 45 minutes
Refrigerate: 20 minutes
Freeze: 15 minutes
Bake: 20 minutes

½ cup salted butter, softened
¼ cup plus 2 tablespoons confectioners' sugar
1 tablespoon light brown sugar
¾ teaspoon vanilla extract, divided
¾ cup all-purpose flour
½ cup chopped toasted sweetened flaked coconut
5 teaspoons cornstarch
⅛ teaspoon salt
⅔ cup plus ½ cup heavy whipping cream, divided
1 (4-ounce) bar semisweet chocolate, such as
   Ghirardelli, chopped
Garnish: toasted sweetened flaked coconut

• Preheat oven to 325°.
• In a medium bowl, combine butter, ¼ cup confectioners' sugar, brown sugar, and ½ teaspoon vanilla extract. Beat at medium speed with an electric mixer until creamy, 1 to 2 minutes.
• In a small bowl, combine flour, coconut, cornstarch, and salt, whisking well. Add flour mixture to butter mixture, beating at low speed until incorporated. Wrap dough in plastic wrap, and refrigerate for 20 minutes.
• Divide dough among 5 (3¾-inch) tartlet pans with removable bottoms, pressing dough into bottoms and up sides of pans. Place tartlet pans on a rimmed baking sheet. Freeze for 15 minutes.
• Prick bottoms of tartlets with a fork to prevent puffing during baking.
• Bake until light golden brown, approximately 20 minutes. Prick again halfway during baking if crusts puff. Let cool completely. (Store in an airtight container at room temperature for up to a day, or freeze for up to a week.)
• In a small saucepan, scald ⅔ cup cream, but do not let it boil. Remove from heat, and add chopped chocolate. Let sit for 1 minute to melt chocolate; stir until smooth and creamy. Pour over cooled crusts, dividing evenly. Let cool.
• In a small bowl, combine remaining ½ cup cream, remaining 2 tablespoons confectioners' sugar, and remaining ¼ teaspoon vanilla extract. Beat at high speed with an electric mixer until stiff peaks form. Transfer whipped cream to a piping bag fitted with a large open-star tip (Wilton #1M). Pipe stars onto surface of cooled tartlets.
• Garnish with coconut, if desired.
• Serve immediately.

Apricot-Glazed White Chocolate Cheesecakes

Yield: 12 mini cheesecakes
Preparation: 30 minutes
Bake: 11 minutes
Refrigerate: 8 hours

¾ cup graham cracker crumbs
3 tablespoons butter, melted
¼ cup plus 1 tablespoon sugar, divided
1 (4-ounce) white chocolate baking bar, such as
   Ghirardelli
1 (8-ounce) package cream cheese, softened
1 large egg
3 teaspoons all-purpose flour
½ teaspoon vanilla extract
Garnish: ⅓ cup apricot jam

• Preheat oven to 350°.
• Spray a 12-well mini cheesecake pan with nonstick cooking spray. Set aside.
• In a small bowl, combine graham cracker crumbs, butter, and 1 tablespoon sugar, stirring well. Divide crumb mixture evenly among wells of prepared pan, pressing to form a level base.
• Bake until golden brown, approximately 6 minutes. Let cool completely.
• Melt white chocolate according to package directions. Set aside.
• In a medium bowl, beat cream cheese at medium speed with an electric mixer until creamy. Reduce speed to low. Add egg, remaining ¼ cup sugar, flour, and vanilla extract, beating until combined. Add melted white chocolate, beating until incorporated. Divide cream-cheese mixture evenly among wells of prepared pan.
• Bake until cheesecakes are set and slightly puffed, approximately 11 minutes. Let cool completely. Refrigerate, covered, for 8 hours or overnight.
• Remove cheesecakes from pan. Top each cheesecake evenly with apricot jam, if desired.

IMPROVISING A THREE-TIER TRAY

If you don't have a three-tier tray for displaying scones, savories, and sweets at your next tea party, don't panic. There are clever ways to improvise this elegant serving piece.

• Stacking ceramic or glass cake plates, as shown above, is a possibility. Many vendors now offer cake plates in graduated sizes that are perfect for this technique. Purchasing the set serves a dual purpose: You get three cake plates of different sizes you can use individually or stack together when you're serving tea.

• If matching cake plates are not available, consider using similar styles but different patterns together—for example, three cut-glass cake plates of varying styles or three ceramic cake plates of different colors. And don't hesitate to borrow a cake plate from your friends or family if you don't own enough.

• If you have a treasured china pattern, Replacements, Ltd., the china-matching service in Greensboro, North Carolina, will make a three-tier tray for you, using three sizes of plates—usually a dinner plate, a salad plate, and a bread-and-butter plate. For more information, call 1-800-REPLACE (1-800-737-5223), or go to *replacements.com*.

German Chocolate–Mascarpone Tartlets

Yield: 24 tartlets
Preparation: 25 minutes
Bake: 10 minutes
Refrigerate: 2 hours

½ cup salted butter, softened
½ cup sugar
1 large egg
½ teaspoon vanilla extract
1½ cups all-purpose flour
½ teaspoon baking powder
¼ teaspoon salt
1 (8-ounce) container mascarpone cheese
1 (4-ounce) German's sweet chocolate bar, such as Baker's, melted according to package directions
Garnish: fresh raspberries, fresh mint

• Preheat oven to 375°.
• Spray a 24-well mini muffin pan with nonstick cooking spray. Set aside.
• In a medium bowl, combine butter and sugar. Beat at medium speed with an electric mixer until creamy. Add egg and vanilla extract, beating to combine. Set aside.
• In a small bowl, combine flour, baking powder, and salt, whisking well. Gradually add flour mixture to butter mixture, beating until combined.
• Divide dough into 1-inch balls. Press into wells of prepared pan, forming tartlet shells.
• Bake until edges of tartlet shells are light golden brown, approximately 10 minutes. Using a rounded spoon, immediately shape warm tartlet shells again by pressing down centers. Let cool in pan for 5 minutes. Carefully remove from pan, and let cool completely on a wire rack. Store in an airtight container for up to a day.
• In a medium bowl, combine mascarpone cheese and melted chocolate, stirring vigorously until smooth and creamy. Refrigerate in a covered container until chocolate mixture is cold and reaches the desired consistency for piping, approximately 2 hours.
• Transfer chocolate mixture to a piping bag fitted with an open-star tip (Wilton #32). Pipe evenly into tartlet shells in a decorative swirl.
• Garnish with fresh raspberries and mint, if desired.
• Serve immediately.

MAKE-AHEAD TIP: *Tartlet shells can be made a week in advance and frozen in an airtight container. Chocolate mascarpone mixture can be made a day in advance and refrigerated in a covered container overnight.*

Apple-Pecan Mini Bundt Cakes
Yield: 12 mini cakes
Preparation: 35 minutes
Bake: 15 minutes

1¼ cups all-purpose flour
½ teaspoon baking soda
½ teaspoon ground cinnamon
¼ teaspoon salt
½ cup plus 2 tablespoons salted butter, softened
¾ cup sugar
1 large egg
1 tablespoon vanilla extract
1 cup (¼-inch) chopped, peeled Golden Delicious
　 apple
½ cup chopped toasted pecans
1 recipe Caramel Glaze (recipe follows)
Garnish: finely chopped toasted pecans and apple
　 slices

• Preheat oven to 350°.
• Spray a 12-well mini Bundt cake pan* with nonstick baking spray with flour. Set aside.
• In a medium bowl, combine flour, baking soda, cinnamon, and salt, whisking well. Set aside.
• In a large bowl, combine butter and sugar. Beat at high speed with an electric mixer until light and fluffy, approximately 3 minutes. Add egg and vanilla extract, beating to combine. Add flour mixture to butter mixture, beating at medium speed for 2 minutes. Add apple and pecans, stirring until incorporated. (Batter will be thick.)
• Divide batter evenly among wells of prepared pans, filling each well three-fourths full. Pat to level.
• Bake until a wooden pick inserted in the centers of cakes comes out clean, approximately 15 minutes. Let cakes cool in pans for 10 minutes. Invert onto wire racks, and let cool completely.

• Working quickly, spoon Caramel Glaze over cooled cakes.
• Garnish cakes evenly with pecans, if desired.
• Store in an airtight container at room temperature when glaze is dry.

*We used a Wilton 12-Cavity Mini Fluted Muffin Pan.

MAKE-AHEAD TIP: *Apple-Pecan Mini Bundt Cakes can be made a day in advance. Store in an airtight container at room temperature.*

Caramel Glaze
Yield: 1¾ cups
Preparation: 15 minutes

½ cup salted butter
1 cup firmly packed light brown sugar
⅔ cup whole milk, divided
1½ cups sifted confectioners' sugar
1 teaspoon vanilla extract

• In a medium saucepan, melt butter over medium heat. Add brown sugar and ⅓ cup milk. Bring to a boil over medium-high heat, stirring constantly. Boil for 2 minutes, stirring constantly. Remove from heat. Add confectioners' sugar and vanilla extract, stirring vigorously and quickly until glaze is smooth and creamy. Add remaining ⅓ cup milk, stirring quickly to incorporate. Add more milk, if necessary, to achieve a very thin glaze.
• Use immediately.

appear on cupcakes. (Stencil cupcakes no more than an hour before serving.)

*We used Wilton Silver Foil Baking Cups, available at wilton.com.

†We used Doily Lace Cake and Cupcake Stencils from Martha Stewart Crafts, available at eksuccessbrands.com/marthastewartcrafts.

MAKE-AHEAD TIP: *Cupcakes can be baked a day in advance and stored in an airtight container to let flavor develop. Stencil cupcakes no more than a hour before serving.*

Chocolate-Cherry Stenciled Cupcakes

Yield: 18 cupcakes
Preparation: 45 minutes
Bake: 20 minutes
Cool: 1 hour

2 cups cake flour
¾ cup sugar
¼ cup natural unsweetened cocoa powder
1¼ teaspoons baking powder
¾ teaspoons baking soda
¾ cup mayonnaise, such as Hellman's
1 teaspoon vanilla extract
¾ cup water
½ cup dried cherries
½ cup semisweet chocolate morsels
Garnish: 1½ cups confectioner's sugar

• Preheat oven to 350°.
• Line 18 wells of 2 (12-well) standard muffin pans with silver foil liners*. Set aside.
• In a large bowl, combine flour, sugar, cocoa, baking powder, and baking soda, whisking well. Add mayonnaise and vanilla extract, beating at low speed with an electric mixer until incorporated. Add water, ¼ cup at a time, beating at low speed. Increase speed to medium and beat for 1 minute. Add dried cherries and chocolate morsels, stirring to combine.
• Divide batter evenly among wells of prepared pans.
• Bake until a wooden pick inserted in the centers of cupcakes comes out clean, approximately 20 minutes. Let cool in pans for 5 minutes. Transfer cupcakes to wire racks, and let cool completely.
• Place a flowered stencil† atop each cupcake, and sift enough confectioners' sugar for stencil pattern to

Orange–Vanilla Bean Zabaglione

Yield: 4 to 6 servings
Preparation: 20 minutes
Cook: 13 minutes
Refrigerate: 4 hours

5 large egg yolks
¼ cup plus 1 tablespoon sugar
1 tablespoon fresh orange zest
¼ cup fresh orange juice
2 tablespoons Marsala wine
1 tablespoon orange-flavored liqueur, such as Grand Marnier Cordon Rouge
1 vanilla bean, split, seeds scraped and reserved
½ cup cold heavy whipping cream
1 tablespoon confectioners' sugar
Garnish: orange curls

• In the top half of a double boiler, combine egg yolks and sugar, whisking until pale. Add orange zest, orange juice, Marsala, orange-flavored liqueur, and reserved vanilla bean seeds. Cook over simmering water, whisking constantly until mixture thickens and a smooth, creamy custard forms, approximately 13 minutes. Remove top half of double boiler, and set into a bowl of ice water to cool, whisking often.
• In a small bowl, combine cream and confectioners' sugar. Beat at high speed with an electric mixer until soft peaks form. Gently whisk whipped cream into cooled custard until smooth and creamy.
• Serve immediately or refrigerate until cold, approximately 4 hours.
• Garnish individual servings with an orange curl, if desired.

KITCHEN TIP: *If you don't have a double boiler, a heatproof bowl (stainless steel or glass) set over a large saucepan of simmering water also works well.*

Salted Caramel Petits Fours

Yield: 100 petit fours
Preparation: 1 hour
Bake: 18 minutes
Freeze: 6 hours
Set: 1 hour

1 cup salted butter, softened
1¾ cups sugar
4 large eggs
3 cups cake flour
3 teaspoons baking powder
½ teaspoon salt
1 cup whole milk
1½ teaspoons vanilla, butter, and nut flavoring, such
  as McCormick
4 recipes Caramel Icing (recipe follows)
Garnish: fleur de sel (French salt)

• Preheat oven to 350°.
• Line a 17-x-12-inch rimmed baking sheet with parchment paper. Spray with nonstick cooking spray. Set aside.
• In a large bowl, combine butter and sugar. Beat at high speed with an electric mixer until light and fluffy, approximately 5 minutes. Add eggs, one at a time, beating at low speed just until incorporated. Set aside.
• In a medium bowl, combine flour, baking powder, and salt, whisking well. Set aside.
• In a measuring cup, combine milk and flavoring.
• Add flour mixture to butter mixture in thirds, alternately with milk mixture, beginning and ending with flour mixture. Beat at low speed to incorporate. Pour batter into prepared pan, and smooth surface with a spatula. Rap pan on the countertop several times to eliminate air bubbles.
• Bake until edges of cake are golden brown and a wooden pick inserted in the center comes out clean, approximately 18 minutes. Let cake cool completely in pan. Wrap tightly with plastic wrap, and freeze for 6 hours or overnight.
• Remove frozen cake from pan. Place on a large wire rack set over a rimmed baking sheet. Using a long serrated knife, trim and discard edges of cake. Line up edges of cake with grid of wire rack. Using grid as a guide, cut cake into 1¼-inch squares. Leave cakes on wire rack to thaw before glazing. (Cakes must be completely thawed and at room temperature for glaze to set properly.)

• Working quickly, spoon Caramel Icing over cakes.
• Garnish with fleur de sel, if desired.
• Let cakes set on cooling rack for 1 hour. Place in decorative paper cups, and store in an airtight container.

KITCHEN TIP: *When glazing petit fours, work with 1 recipe of Caramel Icing and only 25 cake squares at a time. Icing sets up quickly, and it is possible to work only in small batches successfully.*

MAKE-AHEAD TIP: *Cake layer can be baked, wrapped tightly in plastic wrap, and frozen in pan for up to a week in advance. Cut and ice cakes as described above no more than a day in advance. Store at room temperature.*

Caramel Icing

Yield: 2 cups
Preparation: 10 minutes

1 cup salted butter
1 cup firmly packed light brown sugar
⅓ cup whole milk
1½ cups sifted confectioners' sugar
1 teaspoon vanilla extract

• In a medium saucepan, melt butter over low heat. Add brown sugar and milk, stirring to combine. Increase heat to medium high, and bring mixture to a boil, stirring constantly. Boil for exactly 2 minutes, continuing to stir constantly. Remove from heat. Add confectioners' sugar and vanilla extract, whisking until incorporated. Add more milk, if necessary, to achieve desired pourable consistency. (Icing should be thin enough to pour over cakes but thick enough to cover.)
• Use immediately.

"A 'tea,' even though it
be formal, is nevertheless
friendly and inviting."

—Emily Post

Guide TO Steeping Tea

The quality of the tea served at a tea party is as important as the food and the décor. To be sure your infusion is successful every time, here are some basic guidelines to follow.

WATER

Always use the best water possible. If the water tastes good, so will your tea. Heat the water on the stove top or in an electric kettle to the desired temperature. A microwave oven is not recommended.

TEMPERATURE

Heating the water to the correct temperature is arguably one of the most important factors in making a great pot of tea. Pouring boiling water on green, white, and oolong tea leaves can result in a very unpleasant brew. Always refer to the tea purveyor's packaging for specific instructions, but in general, use 170° to 195° water for these delicate tea types. Reserve boiling (212°) water for black and puerh teas, as well as herbal and fruit tisanes.

TEAPOT

If the teapot you plan to use is delicate, warm it with hot tap water first to avert possible cracking. Discard this water before adding the tea leaves or tea bags.

TEA

Use the highest-quality tea you can afford, whether loose leaf or prepackaged in bags or sachets. Remember that these better teas can often be steeped more than once. When using loose-leaf tea, generally use 1 generous teaspoon of dry leaf per 8 ounces of water, and use an infuser basket. For a stronger infusion, add another teaspoonful or two of dry tea leaf.

TIME

As soon as the water reaches the correct temperature for the type of tea, pour it over the leaves or tea bag in the teapot, and cover the pot with a lid. Set a timer—usually 1 to 2 minutes for whites and oolongs; 2 to 3 minutes for greens; and 3 to 5 minutes for blacks, puerhs, and herbals. (Steeping tea longer than recommended can yield a bitter infusion.) When the timer goes off, remove the infuser basket or the tea bags from the teapot.

ENJOYMENT

For best flavor, serve the tea as soon as possible. Keep the beverage warm atop a lighted warmer or under your favorite tea cozy if necessary.

How-tos

Let these step-by-step photos serve as your visual guide while you
create these impressive and delicious teatime treats for your next party.

MANGO ROSE
from Mango-Coconut
Cream Tartlets

Page 36

1. Using a sharp knife, cut mango
slices lengthwise into very thin
(⅛-inch) slices.

2. Roll 1 mango slice into a tight
curl to form the center of a rose.

3. Working out from the center,
add mango slices of varying
lengths in concentric circles to
resemble a rose.

4. Gently slide a thin-blade
spatula under mango rose, and
transfer rose to prepared tartlet.

5. Brush mango rose with
reserved mango syrup.

6. Garnish with fresh mint,
if desired.

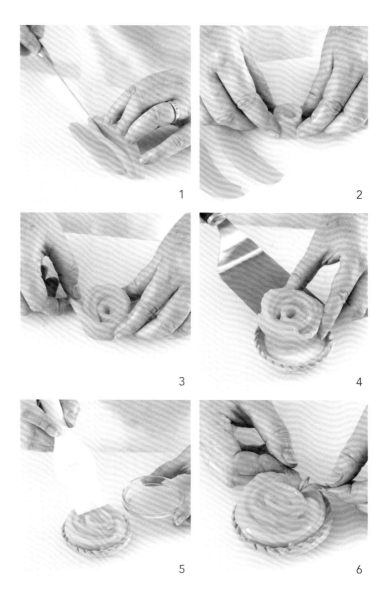

STRAWBERRY RUFFLE CAKES

Page 46

1

Fill a piping bag fitted with a small petal tip (Ateco #101) with Strawberry Buttercream (page 46).

2

With wider end of tip toward bottom, pipe vertical rows of ruffles around sides of cakes, starting at bottom and working upward.

3

Beginning at the edge of cake top, pipe a ruffled circle.

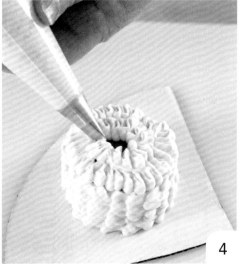

4

Continue piping concentric ruffles, closing up center of circle.

SALMON ROSE
from Salmon Rose
Puffs

Page 78

1. Cut 3-inch strips from smoked salmon.

2. Roll each salmon strip into a rosebud shape, flaring out edges.

3. Place salmon rose inside pastry squares.

4. Roll a slice of pickled ginger into a tight rosebud shape, and place inside salmon rose. Garnish with watercress sprigs.

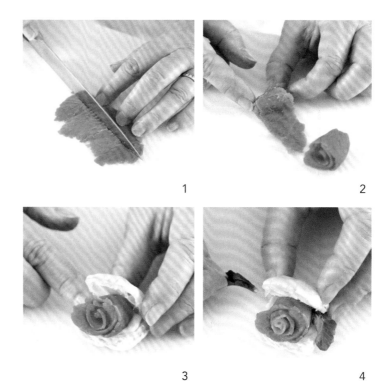

1

2

3

4

TOMATO ROSE
from Tomato Rose
with Shrimp
Couscous Salad

Page 98

1. Using a small serrated knife, cut several overlapping diagonal slits in each Campari tomato.

2. Remove top of tomato.

3. Using the tip of knife, core tomato.

4. Insert knife into slits again, and wiggle it gently to create "petals." Tomato rose is now ready for filling.

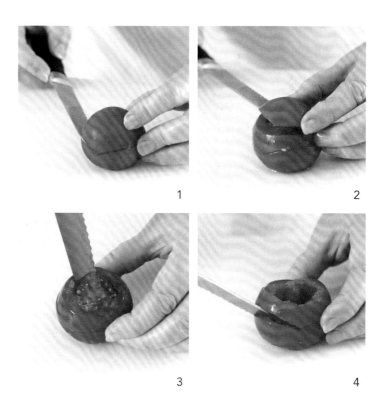

1

2

3

4

Acknowledgments

Recipe development and food styling by Janet Lambert
Photo styling by Lucy W. Herndon

COVER
Photography by Marcy Black Simpson
Floral arrangement by Flowerbuds, 205-970-3223, *flowerbudsinc*. Schuman/Bavaria *Empress Dresden Flowers* 5-piece place setting, teapot, creamer, and sugar*. Godinger *Dublin* 3-tier serving rack from Macy's, *macys.com*.

VALENTINE'S DAY
Photography by Sarah Arrington
Robert Haviland and C. Parlon *Chandigarh* 5-piece place setting, teapot, creamer, and sugar and *Elizabeth* 5-piece place setting from Mottahedeh, 800-443-8225, *mottahedeh.com*. Great White tiered stand†. White buffet tablecloth from World Market, 877-967-5362, *worldmarket.com*. Pom Pom at Home *Audrey* napkins, see pompomathome.com for retailers. Juliska *Berry and Thread* small pitcher, 888-414-8448, *juliska.com*.

EASTER
Photography by Marcy Black Simpson
Floral arrangement by Flowerbuds, 205-970-3223, *flowerbudsinc*. Anchor Hocking cameo-green dinner plate, luncheon plate, and cup and saucer, Tiffin Franciscan *Williamsburg* large basket, and Duncan Miller sandwich clear basket*. Cake Vintage flatware 5-piece place setting from Hester and Cook, 615-385-7254, *hesterandcook.com*. Francesca napkins from Pomegranate Inc., 800-948-5188, *pomegranateinc.com*. Embellished 5-cup silver-plated teapot from Tea for Two, 888-601-9990, *teafortwo.com*.

MOTHER'S DAY
Photography by Marcy Black Simpson
Floral arrangement by Flowerbuds, 205-970-3223, *flowerbudsinc*. Castleton *Sunnyvale* 5-piece place setting, creamer, sugar, and teapot*. Ivory lace napkins and hammered gold napkin rings‡. Godinger *Dublin* 3-tier serving rack from Macy's, *macys.com*. Tablecloth from private collection.

BIRTHDAY
Photography by Sarah Arrington
Floral arrangement by Flowerbuds, 205-970-3223, *flowerbudsinc*. Schuman/Bavaria *Empress Dresden Flowers* 5-piece place setting, teapot, creamer, sugar, and Wedgwood *Ulander Ruby* dinner plate*. Classic linen tablecloth†. Godinger *Dublin* 3-tier server from Belk, 866-235-5443, *belk.com*. Petite Treat

mini pedestals from Rosanna, 877-343-3779, *rosannainc.com*.

CHRISTMAS
Photography by Kamin H. Williams
Floral arrangement by Flowerbuds, 205-970-3223, *flowerbudsinc.com*. Lenox *Winter Greetings* 5-piece place setting, Fitz and Floyd *Renaissance* dark green charger and dinner plate*. 3-Tier Tidbit Tray and two-section bonbon**. Linen hemstitch napkins and place mats in cranberry†.

SCONES
Photography by Sarah Arrington, John O'Hagan, Marcy Black Simpson, and Kamin H. Williams
Page 58: Royal Doulton *Sovereign* bread-and-butter plate and footed cup and saucer*. **Page 59:** Wedgwood *Columbia Gold* teapot*. Small scalloped pedestal from Rosanna, 877-343-3779, *rosannainc.com*. Scalloped white bowl‡. **Page 60:** 3-Tier Tidbit Tray**. **Page 61:** Pewter tiered stand from a private collection. **Page 62:** Royal Crown Derby *Lombardy* bread-and-butter plate, footed cup and saucer, and teapot*. **Page 63:** Wedgwood *Columbia Gold* salad plate and Peony Shape cup and saucer*. **Page 64:** Vintage tiered stand from a private collection. **Page 65:** Royal Doulton *Sovereign* bread-and-butter plate and footed cup and saucer*. **Page 66:** Wedgwood *Ulander Black* bread-and-butter plate and cup and saucer*. Cake Vintage butter spreaders from Hester and Cook, 615-385-7254, *hesterandcook.com*. **Page 67:** Vintage silver stand from a private collection. **Page 68:** Wedgwood *Ulander Gold* bread-and-butter plate and teapot*. **Page 70:** Wedgwood *Colonnade Gold* salad plate, footed cup and saucer, and sugar bowl*. Shimmering glass tiered stand from Pampered Chef, 888-687-2433, *pamperedchef.com*.

SAVORIES
Photography by Sarah Arrington, John O'Hagan, Marcy Black Simpson, and Kamin H. Williams
Page 72: H & C Heinrich *Platinum Scroll* bread-and-butter plate and footed cup and saucer set*. **Pages 73, 83, 98:** Godinger *Dublin* 3-tier server from Belk, 866-235-5443, *belk.com*. **Pages 75, 76, 86:** Circleware *Maison-Clear* 3-piece footed cake tray from Amazon, *amazon.com*. **Pages 77, 85, 87, 89, 95:** 3-Tier Tidbit Tray**. **Pages 78, 84:** White scalloped large cake plate and white scalloped small cake plate‡. **Pages 79, 90, 91, 94:** Shimmering glass tiered stand from Pampered Chef, 888-687-2433, *pamperedchef*

.*com*. **Page 80:** Great White tiered stand†. **Page 81:** H & C Heinrich *Platinum Scroll* bread-and-butter plate and footed cup and saucer set*. **Pages 82, 92, 96, 97:** Pewter tiered stand from a private collection. **Page 88:** Royal Crown Derby *Lombardy* bread-and-butter plate and footed cup and saucer*. **Page 93:** Royal Crown Derby *Lombardy* salad plate and footed cup and saucer*.

SWEETS
Photography by Sarah Arrington, John O'Hagan, Marcy Black Simpson, and Kamin H. Williams
Page 100: Wedgwood *Columbia Gold* teapot, salad plate, and Peony Shape cup and saucer*. **Pages 102, 110:** White scalloped large cake plate‡. **Page 106:** Wedgwood *Colonnade Gold* salad plate and footed cup and saucer*. White cake stand from private collection. **Pages 107, 109, 114:** Shimmering glass tiered stand from Pampered Chef, 888-687-2433, *pamperedchef.com*. **Pages 108, 116, 123:** Circleware *Maison-Clear* 3-piece footed cake tray from Amazon, *amazon.com*. **Pages 111, 119:** Wedgwood *Ulander Gold* bread-and-butter plate and footed cup and saucer*. **Page 113:** Great White tiered stand†. **Pages 115, 122:** Royal Crown Derby *Lombardy* bread-and-butter plate and footed cup and saucer*.

GUIDE TO STEEPING TEA
Photography by Marcy Black Simpson
Page 125: Royal Doulton *Sovereign* footed cup and saucer*.

BACK COVER
Photography by Marcy Black Simpson
Castleton *Sunnyvale* 5-piece place setting, creamer, sugar, and teapot*.

*from Replacements, 800-REPLACE, replacements.com
†from Pottery Barn, 888-779-5176, potterybarn.com
‡from Pier1, 800-245-4595, pier1.com
**from Maryland China, 800-638-3880, marylandchina.com

SPECIALTY TEA PURVEYORS
The teas recommended in each of the menus are available from one or more of these fine companies.
Capital Teas, 888-484-8327, *capitalteas.com*
Grace Tea Company, 978-635-9500, *gracetea.com*
Harney & Sons, 888-427-6398, *harney.com*
Simpson & Vail, 800-282-8327, *svtea.com*
Tealuxe, 888-832-5893, *tealuxe.com*
Teas Etc, 800-832-1126, *teasetc.com*

Recipe Index

"It is the personal
choices and individual
creative touches to
the tiered stand that
make teatime such a
timeless pleasure."

—Jane Pettigrew